IMPLEMENTATION
THE KEY TO SUCCESSFUL
INFORMATION SYSTEMS

IMPLEMENTATION
THE KEY TO SUCCESSFUL
INFORMATION SYSTEMS

HENRY C. LUCAS, JR.

Columbia University Press
New York   1981

Library of Congress Cataloging in Publication Data

Lucas, Henry C.
  Implementation: the key to successful information systems.

  Bibliography: p.
  Includes index.
  1. Management information systems.
2. Business--Data processing. 3. System Analysis.
I. Title.
HF5548.2.L316   658.4'038   80-27009
ISBN 0-231-04434-8

Columbia University Press
New York   Guildford, Surrey

Copyright © 1981 Columbia University Press
Printed in the United States of America

TO ELLEN

CONTENTS

PREFACE

DURING THE LAST three decades organizations have developed and installed computer-based information systems at an incredible rate. The development of these systems has not been confined to large organizations; rapid price reductions for computer hardware have made it possible for the small organization to adopt computer-based information processing as well. Unfortunately, our understanding of how to successfully implement information systems lags far behind our understanding of their technology.

We have seen many information systems which a panel of experts would undoubtedly rate technical successes. However, upon talking to users in the organization we hear a different story. Users criticize systems that on the surface appear to make a positive contribution to the organization; in many instances they do not use the systems at all.

In the first part of this monograph I define implementation and establish criteria for determining the success of an information system. My focus is on implementation as a process which occurs during the entire system life cycle, not merely the last two weeks prior to the conversion of a computer system!

Our limited knowledge of implementation comes from several types of research plus the experiences of a number of individuals who have attempted to implement computer-based information systems. In the first chapter I present a framework for classifying research about implementation to guide the discussion in the next three chapters.

Chapters 2 and 3 of the monograph discuss two types of implementation research: theories and factor research; in chapter 4 I review process studies. Chapter 5 attempts to synthesize the two major research paradigms: factor and process studies. The framework developed helps explain the research studies and offers guidance for implementation. Chapter 6 applies the framework for implementation from chapter 5 to two case studies of the implementation process. My purpose is to show how the framework can be used to analyze the results of an implementation effort.

Unfortunately, I cannot specify a formula for implementation success. The goal of this text is to make the reader aware of the critical importance of implementation in the development of successful information systems and to organize our existing knowledge of this phenomenon. Hopefully through awareness of these issues and by consciously developing a plan for implementation, the reader will be able to improve the chances for successful implementation and successful information systems.

The work of a number of researchers has made this text possible as has the cooperation of numerous subjects of implementation research. I would like to acknowledge the cooperation of colleagues working in this field in furnishing advanced copies of articles and critical comments. Jon Turner at New York University provided extensive assistance and valuable advice. I also acknowledge the support of my wife and best colleague, Ellen, whose encouragement and enthusiasm have made the greatest contribution of all to the monograph.

IMPLEMENTATION
THE KEY TO SUCCESSFUL
INFORMATION SYSTEMS

CHAPTER ONE

THE NATURE OF IMPLEMENTATION RESEARCH

IT IS APPARENT that many computer-based information systems have failed. Either these systems are not used at all or have not achieved their potential. Users complain about the information they receive and the quality of information processing services. Top management complains that its large investments in expensive computer-based information systems seem to have no return for the organization. Is the development of information systems any different than other projects undertaken by the organization? Information systems have several characteristics that make them dissimilar from other projects such as building a new plant.

Frequently the development of a system involves research and development: it is not always clear that what is being proposed for a system is feasible. Systems also deal with intangibles; information is hard to define. The same data are interpreted differently by different individuals who define the information content of the date. Users must supply complete and accurate input if a system is to succeed. Systems also usually have a vital function for the entire organization or a major part of it; they supply information for decision making and control. A crucial characteristic of most information systems is that individuals are asked or required to change their behavior to make the system function. I shall explore this key aspect of systems further in the chapter. While an organization may undertake many projects, the development of information systems is important. One objective of this book is to provide an understanding of how we may improve the chances for successful information systems development.

Several examples below illustrate some of the problems encountered in the development of these systems:

- In one case the information services department manager for a manufacturing company was asked to provide examples of the reports produced by his department. The manager responded that it would be easy to do so because he had not distributed the reports for the prior month: "they had not looked exactly right." The most disturbing aspect of this example was the fact that users had not noticed the missing reports.

- In another situation a university on-line system was developed to store and retrieve information about administration and operations within the university. The on-line system featured a complex Boolean retrieval language. However, the system was available only on a limited basis and frequently ceased functioning during the time it was supposedly available due to program problems. There was extreme user dissatisfaction with this system particularly when compared with the university's old traditional batch processing systems.

- In another example a mining company developed a successful system in one division to manage a large inventory of spare parts. However, the division managers in other divisions successfuly resisted the installation of the system in their locations despite the fact that cost savings could be demonstrated.

- As a final example the vice president of a major bank immediately threw all mail with computer printouts in a wastebasket without even glancing at it.

These and other instances suggest that there are many problems with existing computer-based information systems. The design and implementation of computer applications is generally considered to be a technical task. Most of the systems above worked technically; the reports in the manufacturing company were produced. The only real technical problem was frequent machine failure. In the university case the system was very elegant technically; there were bugs in the individual programs, but the technical design was very advanced. In the mining company example the system was good from a technical standpoint; it included sophisticated demand forecasting models and an economic order quantity model. The bank vice president's behavior can probably be explained by past problems with systems. Possibly some of these problems were due to technical difficulties, but the bank vice president has generalized from isolated experiences to all systems.

Based on research, my conclusion is that technical quality is a necessary, but not sufficient, condition for successful systems. Technical quality can not be defined solely by the criteria of the computer scientist, but rather the functions of the system as seen by the user determine technical quality. Technical quality also means reliable service: systems must be available and must meet processing schedules. Systems must also be capable of being maintained so that processing can be provided over time as changes are needed to correct errors or add enhancements.

If technical quality is not the only factor, what else influences the success of an information system? This book explores the issues which must be considered for successful implementation. In the next section we look at the nature of information systems and a possible measure of success. Then I discuss the basic themes of research on implementation and the nature of research in the field.

Chapter 2 presents several theories of the implementation

process and chapters 3 and 4 discuss results from implementation research studies. Chapter 5 presents a conceptual framework of implementation which attempts to synthesize different approaches to the study of implementation. This model can be used to guide the implementation of an information system or an operations research model. In chapter 6 I examine two case studies to show how the framework can be used for analysis and for planning implementation.

This text is intended for two types of readers. The first is the thoughtful designer or user concerned with how to successfully implement on information systems. The second type of reader is the researcher who would like a review and synthesis of major implementation research. It is hoped that the ideas contained here will be helpful to both kinds of readers.

THE NATURE OF INFORMATION SYSTEMS

Definition

Information systems provide information to support decision making and control in the organization. Information itself is some tangible or intangible entity which reduces our uncertainty about a state or event. As an example, consider a weather forecast that it will be clear and sunny tomorrow. This forecast reduces uncertainty in making a decision whether to have a picnic tomorrow. The degree to which uncertainty is reduced is proportional to our faith in the accuracy of the weather forecast.

Information is used for control purposes in the organization as well as decision-making. For example, information on raw materials and work in process inventories is needed for production control purposes in a manufacturing plant. Similarly, information on orders and forecasts along with plant capacity are required to schedule production. In this way information systems serve to help control the organization and to support decisions.

Frameworks

It is helpful to have a common basis for thinking about and discussing an information system. A framework is a conceptual model which facilitates discussions about systems. One of the most useful frameworks for decision making was developed by Robert Anthony (1965). Anthony's framework focuses on decisions and is very appropriate given the information systems often exist to support decision making. Anthony's framework is also important because it distinguishes different information requirements associated with different types of decisions.

Anthony (1965).   Anthony defines three types of decisions. The first of these is strategic planning which is the process of deciding on the objectives of the organization and on the resources needed to attain these objectives. Strategic planning is generally associated with long range decisions which are made infrequently. The next category, managerial control decisions, involve problems primarily of a personnel and financial nature. Managerial control is a process through which managers assure that adequate resources are available and that these resources are used effectively to accomplish the objectives of the organization. Anthony's final decision category is operational control. Decisions in this area deal with specific tasks which must be carried out efficiently. Operational control decisions are concerned with the day-to-day operations of the firm.

Experience has shown that it is necessary to add one more category to the Anthony scheme and that is transactions processing. Many, if not most, computer-based systems have been designed to process transactions. These systems feature almost no decision making information; they automate paper processing much as the assembly line automated manufacturing. Transactions systems are some of the most critical to the organization. These basic systems must function properly before one can worry about corporate strategy or long range planning.

The Anthony categories have been presented as discrete,

though they really are continuous. It is generally not possible to classify a single decision exclusively in one category. However, the Anthony framework is useful in providing a general descriptive model of decisions and the nature of information associated with these decision types. See table 1.1.

Simon (1965).   Simon suggests another framework; he distinguishes between structured and unstructured activities. Structured decisions are those which are capable of being programmed, that is, we can specify a set of procedures to be followed to make a decision. An unstructured decision problem occurs when the situation defies the application of prespecified rules and procedures.

Gorry and Scott Morton (1971).   The authors have combined the Anthony and the Simon models to form a combined framework for information systems. Their approach in figure 1.1 arrays the Anthony decision-types as columns of a table and structured, semistructured, and unstructured categories of decisions as the rows. This framework combines the decision-oriented approaches with application-oriented frameworks and is very helpful in suggesting new directions for the design of computer-based information systems. Most applications today fall into the structured, operational control cell of the framework such as accounts receivable, payroll, and inventory control. (These are really transactions rather than operational systems.) As more of these systems are implemented, the trend for new applica-

Table 1.1   Information Requirements for Decision Types

Characteristic of Information	Operational Control	Management Control	Strategic Planning
Decision maker	Foremen, clerks		Top management
Source	Largely internal		Largely external
Complexity	Simple		Complex
Level of aggregation	Detailed		Aggregated, summary
Frequency of reporting	Frequent		Infrequent

Classification	Decision Purpose		
	Operational Control	Management Control	Strategic Planning
Decision Type			
Structured	Order processing	Budgets	Warehouse location
	Accounts payable	Personnel reports	Transportation mode mix
Semistructured	Inventory control	Analysis of variance	Introduction of new product
Unstructured	Cash management	Management of personnel	Planning of R&D

Figure 1.1   The Gorry and Scott Morton Information Systems Framework
SOURCE: Courtesy of McGraw-Hill.

tions will be to occupy cells in the lower right-hand side of figure 1.1. We expect computer-based information systems to support more managerial control and strategic planning decisions and less structured decisions in general.

Each axis of this framework represents a continuum, so it is difficult to make rigid classifications. Systems themselves may have output which falls into one or more cells of the table. As we move into unstructured areas the line separating unstructured applications from those which are highly structured will probably tend to move. Some experts maintain that decisions can no longer be classified as anything but structured once an information system has been developed. This fine distinction is not too important, but the trend that it suggests is significant. Computer-based information systems should provide more structured information in areas which have previously been semi-or unstructured. Such systems will probably not actually make decisions, but instead will provide different types of information and organize it for the decisionmaker, helping him or her develop new insights into problems.

Gorry and Scott Morton speculate that most information systems have been rather mundane. Structured operational control decisions have been automated first in most companies, and these authors predict that new systems will attack unstructured problems. However, if users are dissatisfied with present systems which are relatively simple, the implementation of more sophisticated systems is not likely to be successful either. The question of implementation becomes even more salient in dealing with systems to support decision making. There will most probably be a movement toward more computer-based information systems to support the sophisticated and complex decisions in managerial control and strategic planning.

Type of Use

Another important characteristic of information systems is the way in which they are used. A voluntary system is one in which the user has discretion in employing the system. Most decision-oriented systems are voluntary: the user can decide not to use the system.

For transactions processing and operational systems, those responsible for input usually have no choice; they must provide the input as a part of their jobs. However, a manager may choose to use or ignore a report generated by one of these systems. Thus, there may be both voluntary and required use of the same system.

Designers need to consider how to encourage voluntary use; there is no quarantee that because designers or some managers rate a system highly that all potential users will take advantage of it. Even when the use of a system can be required as a part of someone's job, we must still be careful, as forced use of a poorly designed system can lead to alienation and even sabotage of the system.

Impact on the Organization

Understanding the potential impact of a system can help in planning its development. An information system can have an impact on the structure of an organization, groups of individuals, and individuals.

The structure of an organization may be altered due to a new system or because a system made changes possible. One firm had several different departments with concerns for customer service, one for retail and one for wholesale customers. A new computer-based system will make information available in one place so the firm is planning to create a new department responsible for all customer service. This represents a major change in organizational structure; several functions will be reorganized.

In the example above, work groups will also be changed. Different groups will be moved to new departments. It is quite likely that some individuals will become members of new work groups. This restructuring of group membership occurs frequently when information systems are developed.

Finally for almost every information system, users must learn something new. Users have to contend with some new input in terms of content, format, and/or medium of entry. Output is also frequently different after a new system is installed.

These inpacts on the organization may also affect the distribution of power in the organization. Power is the ability to influence behavior and outcomes. A system may provide information which is related to power since information reduces uncertainty. Coping with uncertainty is associated with high power (Hickson et al. 1971) Systems also create new levels of interdependence in the organization, often between user and computer departments. If one unit depends on another, it is less powerful than when independent. Power in organizations may also be thought of according to the level of responsibility and the size of an operation. Changes in organizational structure can alter this distribution of power.

One common theme of the impacts discussed above is change. We develop a new information system because we wish to change existing information processing procedures. These changes may have an impact on the structure of the organization, the work group, individuals and the distribution of power. We have not seen a system which did not affect one or all of these components of the organization.

Information Systems and Operations Research Models

Much of the literature on implementation relates to operations research/management science (OR/MS) models. These models are generally of a mathematical nature and can be divided into several groups. Optimizing models suggest the solution which is best mathematically. Examples of optimizing models include economic order quantity calculations, linear programs, etc. Of course, a model is only optimal given the quality of the assumptions and data. The simplest economic order quantity models, for example, assume deterministic demand and are not concerned with buffer stocks or probabilistic usage during lead time. Adding such considerations requires a more complex model and the optimum solution will undoubtedly differ from the optimum of the simpler model.

Another class includes simulation models; a number of runs are made and the best observation is chosen. There is no guarantee that the best solution is optimum and another simulation would not differ. Changing some aspects of the model or data might produce better results.

Forecasting models are used to predict future events, such as sales, the position of the economy, etc. These models usually involve the use of historical data and may involve the extrapolation from or smoothing of these data.

How do these models relate to information systems; what are the similarities and differences? See table 1.2. An information system is an abstract model of information processing in the organization. Both systems and models are abstractions of something intangible when compared to the model of a building constructed by an architect. The information systems model, however, is usually not as complex mathematically as an op-

Table 1.2 Typical Information Systems and OR Model Characteristics

	Information Systems	OR Models
User	Broad range	One person or small group
Complexity	Technologically complex	Mathematically complex
Decision support	Small role; often transactions processing	Decision-oriented
Type	Deterministic, one alternative	Optimizing, simulation, several alternatives considered

erations research model. The information system, though, is likely to be technically complex in terms of computer technology and the software required to support the application.

Operations research models do provide information for decisionmakers and thus they are information systems in their own right. Often OR models are a part of a larger information system such as an EOQ model embedded in an inventory control system. Some OR practitioners, recognizing the assumptions in their models, suggest that optimizing models provide only one possible solution and the results of several different models are often presented to the decisionmaker.

Thus, there are many similarities between OR/MS models and computer-based information systems: an OR model is usually an information system or at least a component of an information system. We can use the results of research on the implementation of OR/MS models to help us understand better the implementation of computer-based information systems.

WHAT IS SUCCESS?

There are a number of possible indicators of successful information systems which have been suggested by various studies of implementation. Unless a set of success measures is agreed upon it will be difficult to evaluate the quality of systems. While not a new problem, it is still a perplexing one. Dickson and Powers (1973) surveyed a group of information systems experts about what factors contribute to success. The authors factor analyzed the results of the questionnaire, and correlated the factors with four different success criteria:

1. Time to complete the project/time estimated to complete
2. Actual cost to develop project/budgeted cost for the project
3. User satisfaction; managerial attitudes toward the system and how well their information needs were satisfied
4. The impact of the project on the computer operations of the firm.

The researchers found that these four measures of success were independent when correlated with factors hypothesized to contribute to success.

If various success criteria are not related, then it will be difficult to draw conclusions and generalize from studies that employ these criteria. We shall have to consider various measures for success and consider the results of different studies in light of the success criteria they employ.

For the most part the success measures of Dickson and Powers have not been widely adopted in implementation research with the exception of user satisfaction. Most research has employed one or more of the following measures:

1. The use of the system as measured by intended or actual use, for example, the number of inquiries made of an on-line system;
2. User satisfaction such as self-report measures on a questionnaire or interview;
3. Favorable attitudes, either as an objective alone or as a good predictor of the use of a system;
4. The degree to which a system accomplishes its original objectives;
5. Payoff to the organization from a system; for example through cost reductions, increased sales, etc.

Why has there not been more emphasis on the benefits exceeding the costs as the definition of implementation success? Many textbooks stress a cost/benefit analysis as a basis for selecting information systems projects.

There are three major reasons why cost/benefit analysis is not used more in research on implementation. First, it is difficult to measure the costs, and the benefits of information may not be quantifiable. (However, in general costs are easier to estimate than benefits.) Second, for more advanced systems beyond transactions processing and operational control, savings often cannot be demonstrated with any certainty. For transactions processing systems one can sometimes show savings in labor especially in projecting requirements for labor in the future. An operational control system might show a reduction in inventory which can be converted into a dollar savings. However, how can we evaluate the benefits for a planning model if the recommendations of the model are followed? It is very difficult to determine the benefits from action taken at the suggestion of the model since the action precludes some other option which could be the basis for comparison. If we install an inventory system we continue to have an inventory and balances before and after the implementation of a model can be compared. The divestment of a subsidiary recommended by a planning model changes conditions so much that evaluation is extremely difficult.

Finally, researchers in the field generally feel the most important implementation problems are human and organizational; they are not as likely to include costs and benefits from the system in their research. Cost/benefit measures are difficult to apply because of the problem of developing realistic estimates. A cost/benefit analysis is also incomplete; implementation involves behavioral and organizational considerations, not just economic factors.

Cost/benefit measures are important; however, because of the problems with this measure described above, an indicator of success like use is more appropriate. We cannot adopt use as a measure for all information systems. As discussed above, there are many systems where use is involuntary so there will be little differences among the individuals working with the system. A sales representative has to complete an order form for a computer-based order-entry system for the customer to receive merchandise and for the sales representative to receive a commission. Such a system is involuntary and here we have to use a success criterion like satisfaction.

For the sales manager who receives a sales analysis report from the order entry system, use is an appropriate measure of system success. This manager may use the report extensively or ignore it at his or her discretion.

This book will review studies in which one or more of the indicators of success like those described above were used to evaluate a system. The particular indicator chosen is contingent on the situation and the system in the study. We shall find that no one success measure is uniformly applicable across all implementation efforts. However, we should always be able to define one or more indicators of successful implementation given a particular information system and the context in which it is being implemented. For our purposes most frequently we shall adopt use as a measure of success where use is voluntary and satisfaction where it is not.

What Then is Implementation?

The implementation of a computer-based information system is an on-going process which includes the entire development of the system from the original suggestion through the feasibility study, systems analysis and design, programming, training, conversion, and installation of the system. Many authors refer to implementation only as the final stage in the systems life cycle. The study of implementation also must include organizational change. For this reason much of implementation research is concerned with organizational and individual behavior. Very few systems exist outside of the context of an organization. The theories and research we discuss can best be classified in the field of social science rather than engineering or computer science.

Types of Implementation Research

There are three major types of research and writing about implementation. First, there are theories and proposals, though most of these theories about implementation are not really scientific. I find it difficult to develop testable hypotheses from the theories; they are often informal and describe approaches to implementation. The theorists provide insight and ideas to be used in implementing computer-based information systems. However, there is no guarantee that the suggestions will work. The recommendations from social science are not as precise as the rules of physics.

The book discusses surveys of factors which are important in successful implementation. A large number of factors have been indentified through this type of implementation research, for example, attitudes toward a system, management support, and so on. Factors may be constructed from a single variable, for example, age, or from a series of variables like a group of questionnaire items which assess user attitudes toward a system.

Factors tend to be static and this type of research usually suggests that factor A is associated with B, e.g., management support may be related to a user's intentions to work with a new system. Factor studies are analytical and often are sterile, but rigorous.

There is also research describing the process of implementation often in the form of case studies. Process here means how the system is developed, for example, a description of the relationship among individuals working on a system. This research, unlike factor studies, attempts to probe the way in which a system is developed and examine human relationships. These studies may appear unfocused at times and less rigorous than factor research. However, process studies contribute a great deal to our understanding of the implementation process.

RESEARCH DESIGNS AND METHODOLOGY

Much of the research in the implementation field involves the collection of data to test theories and hypotheses. This approach to research is fairly common in a number of fields like economics, psychology, sociology and other social sciences. In this section we briefly discuss some important criteria to consider in the evaluation of research on implementation. The appendix to this chapter contains a more detailed presentation of research methodology.

The most important criteria that have been employed to select studies for inclusion in this monograph are:

Control over extraneous and confounding variables
The nature of the sample
The interaction of the researcher and instruments
Replicability
Realism
Strength of causal inferences
Generalizability

Of course, there is one overriding criterion which is not included in this list: the research has to present something interesting and relevant for implementation. There are many studies in almost any field which address obscure points or artifical problems. Other times studies do not really provide much information about the phenomenon being studied. I have tried to eliminate such research from this monograph.

In the list above, control over extraneous and confounding variables expresses a concern with the nature of the variables selected for inclusion in a study. Did the researcher omit significant variables which really are responsible for the results observed? Did the researcher include the important variables and consider them adequately?

The nature of the sample selected is important for a study for two reasons. First, the statistical analysis employed in the studies usually assumes random sampling. While this requirement is not often met in social science research one should at least feel that the sample does not differ markedly from a truly random sample. We also want to consider the nature of the sample to decide to what population one can generalize the results. For example, if the sample is a group of college sophmores, does one really want to generalize the results to adults working in a large corporation?

In many empirical studies, there is the possibility that the instruments or the researcher may unintentionally influence the results. In a case study, the researcher may acutally be a participant in an implementation project. How objective can such an individual be in reporting the story of the implementation effort?

Replicability refers to the ability to repeat the findings. If we are to generalize from a study, then the same results should be obtainable in another, similar study. Are the results of the study consistent with other research? Does the design seem of sufficient quality that the results are likely to be repeated in follow-up research?

Realism refers to the credibility of the research setting and is of most concern in laboratory exercises. Often to gain the control of a laboratory experiment, we sacrifice a realistic setting. Lack of realism may make the reader uneasy about applying the findings to a real-life situation.

Much of research is oriented toward finding casual relationships. Is there evidence that variable A causes variable B? If so, then can we manipulate variable A in order to influence B? By increasing user involvement in design can we improve the probability that a user will provide the input demanded by a system? Various types of search provide weak or strong evidence on causality. One must carefully evaluate the researcher's claim of causality in light of the research design.

Finally, there is the extent to which one can generalize the results of the research to other situations. A valuable study should provide as much generalizable knowledge as possible.

IMPLEMENTATION RESEARCH

The last section discribed three types of implementation research studies—theories, factor research, and process research. What are the typical research designs employed for these studies? Theories and essays generally are not considered to be empirical research, they suggest ideas for studies. Table 1.3 shows the predominant characteristics of empirical implementation research. These are the most typical attributes of the two approaches though we shall encounter occasional exceptions and studies that really are a hybrid of several types of research.

Factor studies are most often conducted in the field using survey research techniques. Observations in factor studies usually, but not always, occur at one point in time. The sample may be random within the organization, but the organization was probably not selected randomly itself. Few control groups are present in this type of study. Data sources are likely to be both primary and secondary and data collection is most often through a questionnaire or interview. (Primary data are developed by the researcher; secondary exist already, for example, company records).

Table 1.3 Predominant Characteristics of Empirical Implementation Research

	Factor Studies	Process Studies
Purpose	Identify factors and interrelationships	Understand development of system
Location	Field, laboratory	Field
Observation	Cross-sectional, longitudinal	Longitudinal
Sample	Semi-random	Non-random
Control group	Possible	Usually omitted
Data sources	Primary and secondary	Primary and secondary
Data collection	Questionnaires interviews	Interviews observations

There are other factor studies which have moved into the laboratory to gain control over extraneous variables. This type of design is good to focus on the relationship of one factor to implementation, for example, the cognitive style of the user. Laboratory research generally is experimental with longtudinal observations. Subjects are most often not selected randomly, but are randomly assigned to treatment groups and a control group. Data collection is generally from primary sources though the experiment itself may provide secondary data. Questionnaires and interviews are the most popular instruments for data collection.

Process research in implementation occurs in the field and often is a single case study with non-random selection and a sample size of one (a few exceptions have included data collected systematically from a number of individuals in a single case study). Research of this type is longtudinal, though there are no control groups or extensive data reported in most published studies. Data can be collected from both primary and secondary sources and often come from an observer or a participant observer.

From the stand point of increasing our knowledge about implementation all types of studies are important. Figure 1.2 attempts to diagram how the various types of research are related. Theory usually leads to exploratory case studies whose results are fed back to modify or develop theories. The theories generate both insights and factors for further research.

Factor research helps to validate research models and generally presents a "black box view," that is, a model usually describes what happened, but does not explain well how it happened. Process research through case studies presents rich stories which attempt to explain and interpret what, how and why something happened. The factor study provides strong evidence for or against relationships hypothesized to exist among factors given the limitations of survey research designs. The process studies, though subject to the biases of the researcher, help explain phenomena, and suggest how to proceed in an implementation effort.

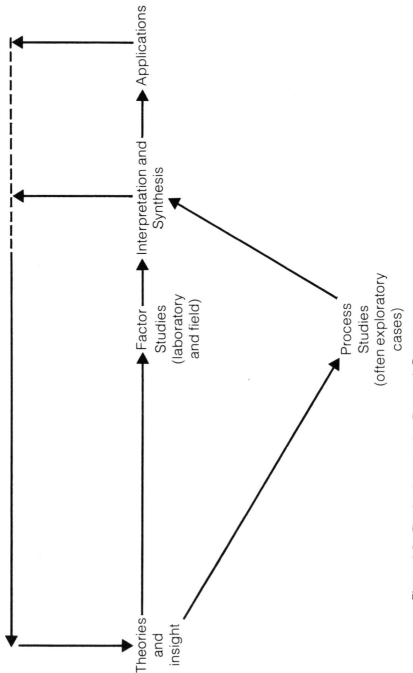

Figure 1.2 The Implementation Research Process

APPENDIX

RESEARCH DESIGNS AND METHODOLOGY

Because of a desire to understand implementation, researchers have gathered data in various forms to test their theories and ideas.

Research Models

It is helpful to distinguish among a number of types of models in discussing empirical research. Descriptive models attempt to explain some phenomenon through a description of the underlying dynamics of a process. Future events are forecast through the use of predictive models; given a set of inputs, what outcome does one expect? A final type of model is normative and suggests the best way to proceed, for example, many operations research models are normative. Provided with a set of assumptions and an objective function these models determine an optimum solution. Research in any field that is empirical usually begins with descriptive models. The researcher collects data and processes them to increase his or her understanding of the relationships among key variables. This descriptive model is modified, refined and validated through repeated studies. When validated a descriptive model is often used for the purposes of prediction. The researcher now has gained an understanding of the relationships between dependent and independent variables through the descriptive model and can predict future outcomes given values of the independent variables.

The implications of valid descriptive and predictive models may be normative, that is, if one has confidence in the relationships among the variables, one may be even suggest normative guidelines for action. However, it is unlikely that these empirical models will ever provide optimum solutions since it is so difficult to state objective functions for the model.

The first task of the model builder is to identify dependent variables. What outcome is of interest? As mentioned, the most popular dependent variables in the study of implementation are attitudes or some measure of actual or intended use of a system. Some of the studies in the text include multiple dependent variables such as intended use and an actual frequency of inquiry for an on-line system. The use of multiple dependent variables offers the advantage of greater reliability, particularly when the variables are measured with data collected from different sources. It is also helpful to have measures that compare self-report data from interviews and questionnaries with actual behavior such as a monitor tracing inquiries made of an on-line system.

An independent variable may in principle be manipulated to influence dependent variables. Simple models include the relationship between one dependent and one independent variable. For example, a researcher might hypothesize that involvement in design leads to high levels of use of an information system. Here use is a dependent variable and involvement is the independent variable.

More complex models include multiple independent variables which are hypothesized to be related to the dependent variable. A reseacher might hypothesize that system use depends on both involvement and the quality of computer-based systems.

The most complex models include intervening variables, that is, there are chains of relationships among variables. A model might propose that involvement improves user attitudes, which in turn lead to high levels of system use. These more complex models are usually quite difficult to validate and place severe requirements on data collection and analysis.

In any research of this type, the researcher is generally trying to demonstrate causality, that is, variable A leads to variable B. However, he or she can never really prove causality conclusively, especially in the social sciences. Instead, a researcher tries to provide evidence supportive of causal relationships through better research designs and multiple studies. One cannot infer causality because two variables are highly correlated. A may cause B, B may cause A or some third variable C may cause both A and B to move together. Therefore one should be very careful in making causal inferences from the research results presented later in the monograph.

Measuring Variables

Models frequently employ classes of variables which must be operationalized. Attitudes toward the system are quite general and we must specify what system and what attitudes are to be measured.

In implementation research there generally are several sources of data. One can collect data through observation, for example, by watching an implementation effort. Through interviews the researcher talks to various individuals to determine their attitudes, role, etc., interviews can be highly structured or very unstructured. Interviews provide an oportunity to explain questions and to follow a trend. However, they are costly and sometimes interviewers can lead a subject and introduce bias.

Questionnaires are generally highly structured. The advantage of the questionnaire is the ability to administer it economically to a large sample. The major disadvantage of questionnaires is the assumption that the questions mean the same thing to each respondent and that the answers encompass all possible responses.

Research Designs

Table 1.4 summarizes several characteristics for classifying different types of research designs on implementation. Such a classifications scheme helps in evaluating research and communicating about different designs.

Table 1.4 Some Popular Research Designs

Location	Field Laboratory
Focus	Survey
	Experimental
Observation	Cross sectional
	Longitudinal
	Time series
Sample	Random
	Non-random
Control group	Existence
Data source	Primary
	Secondary
Data collection	Observer
	Participant
	Questionnaire
	Interview

Empirical studies are either conducted in a field or a laboratory location. Field settings usually include research in an organization and this type of setting has been very popular in implementation research due to its realism. Laboratory research efforts compliment the field study. A researcher has better control over the environment in a laboratory study and the results of this research usually offer stronger evidence on causality than field research. However, it is hard to develop a realistic laboratory setting for implementation studies.

The focus of research designs can be survey or experimental. A large number of individual subjects are involved in survey research, but usually there is no experimental manipulation of the independent variables. A researcher might conduct a study of user attitudes toward a computer system and compare these attitudes with usage data collected from a monitor in the system. In an experiment a researcher might compare two groups before and after the introduction a new computer system. One group uses the new system and the other one does not.

Research designs differ in the method of observation. In cross-sectional research all data are collected at one point at time. This type of observation creates the most difficulties when making causal inferences, because changes in variables are not observed over time. Correlations among variables in cross-sectional research do not show causality, however, correlations show possible causal relations. Sometimes a priori reasoning on the timing of relationships among variables supports causal arguments based on cross-sectional data; for example, if a researcher observes a correlation between chronological age and attitudes, it is fairly safe to assume that age leads to attitudes rather than attitudes lead to age.

The strongest case for causality is from longitudinal studies where data are collected at more than one point in time. Longitudinal studies, however, are difficult to conduct because one must determine the appropriate time interval between measurements. How long does it take for changes in independent variables to create changes in the dependent variables? If questionnaires are employed the researcher does not want such frequent repetition that subjects become irritated. In a laboratory study the researcher cannot always be sure that the treatments has time to affect the subjects.

As stated above, samples can be either random or non-random in the research.

A control group is often used to control for confounding variables. In an experimental study a researcher might use a group for whom there are no changes made in the independent variable to control for variables affecting the subjects unrelated to the experiment and the interaction between the experimentor and the subjects. The researcher when analyzing data would look at changes in the experimental group and compare them with changes in the control group. Cross-sectional survey research generally does not have control groups because of the lack of experimental manipulation of independent variables.

Empirical research can draw on a large number of sources of data. As mentioned earlier it is better to have multiple sources of data whenever possible to improve measurement reliability. Responses to questionnaires may reflect a halo affect in which the respondent answers all questions favorably, because he or she is optimistic that day. If the researcher observes correlations among variables, it may be because of a problem with measurement instruments rather than the presence of an underlying relationship. The presence of multiple sources of data means that there is less chance for this type of incorrect result.

Primary data collection means that a researcher is actually generating the information through a questionnaire, interview or by building a monitor into a computer system. Secondary data have been collected long before the researcher begins a study. An example of secondary data would be company records of changes in number of personnel, system usage measured by an existing computer job accounting system, etc. Secondary data sources provide data inexpensively and the data can be collected more easily than from primary sources.

There are a number of ways to collect data from primary sources. The first is through the observer who remains detached from the situation, while the second is a participant observer who actually participates in the implementation effort. Participant observers may generate biased data because of their role in the implementation effort itself. Questionnaires are another method of primary data collection and are very popular because of their relatively low cost and ease of administration. A final method for primary data collection is to interview subjects. Interviews can be costly though they often lead to more insights than a highly structured questionnaire.

The criteria described above and the classification scheme for research were used to select studies and papers for discussion in the next three chapters of the monograph. An attempt has also been made to include only studies that are highly significant in terms of insight or which demonstrate good research methodology.

CHAPTER TWO
THEORIES AND SUGGESTIONS

THIS CHAPTER REVIEWS theories of implementation. In most disciplines a theory is a statement of how general classes of variables are related to each other. It should be possible to derive testable hypotheses from a theory and conduct research to validate it. In a social science we really do not prove a theory conclusively, but we try to present sufficient evidence that a reasonable observer would agree the theory has validity. If research disproves hypotheses then we should modify the theory and conduct further research.

Why are there so many theories in management compared with the natural sciences? In a social science like business we are dealing with an extremely large number of variables. The possible linkages among them is almost overwhelming. Also, the context of the research differs from the laboratory of the scientist. We conduct field studies and laboratory experiments. However, when we try to apply research results, we find the situation different in each organization. There is a wide variety of contextual variables which influence implementation as will be seen in the next chapter.

We are also dealing with behavioral phenomena; events are perceived by different individuals. The same evidence may lead one researcher to entirely different conclusions than another. In fact, it is often the case that the same data fit many different models. We shall probably never have a single theory of implementation. Instead, our goal should be to adopt an approach which 1) points out the most important variables in implementation; 2) describes general relationships among the variables; and 3) helps to develop an implementation strategy for the design installation of a computer-based information system.

The framework to be presented in chapter 5 has been developed for the above purpose; however, other conceptual models are equally valid. It is most important to have some model in mind which calls attention to the fact that implementation is a change process and relates factors and the change process in some way.

The rest of this chapter discusses a number of theories of implementation, though much of the writing on implementation is difficult to classify as theory according to our definition. The discussion falls into two parts: theories and essays. The theories have been suggested as ways to explain implementation and usually can be tested empirically in some way. (A few of the theories are tested through research studies and the evidence is presented here for completeness' sake rather than in subsequent chapters.) Essays, on the other hand, often present recommendations which are not necessarily related to each other. Usually, the recommendations are offered by individuals acting as participant observers in a large number of mplementation projects and are suggested to other implementors. The theories discussed are summarized in table 2.1.

THEORIES

Mutual Understanding

Churchman and Schainblatt (1965). One of the most frequently cited articles on implementation is entitled "The Researcher and the Manager: A Dialectic of Implementation." The

Table 2.1 Summary of Theories

AUTHOR	FOCUS
Theories	
Churchman and Schainblatt (1965)	Relationship between specialist and user stressing mutual understanding.
Mason and Mitroff (1973)	Variables important in research on information systems including the individual, organizational context, problem type, psychological type and mode of presentation.
Shakun (1972)	Situational normativism including a descriptive model of the real world before constructing a mathematical model.
Zand and Sorensen (1975)	Application of the Lewin change strategy of unfreezing, change, refreezing.
Schultz and Slevin (1977)	An adaptive process model of implementation stressing individual reactions.
Lucas (1974)	Creative Design featuring user control, attention to the user interface and user defined systems quality.
Galbraith (1979)	Indirect diffusion by "adding on" to desired changes.
Bean and Radnor (1979)	Use of intermediaries, especially those related functionally to user.
Observations	
Malcolm (1965)	Recommendations for beginning an OR effort.
Ackoff (1967)	Five popular myths in systems analysis and design.
McCoubrey and Sulg (1976)	Extensive suggestions for how to conduct an OR/MS effort.
Hammond (1974)	Benefits and problems of OR, especially for oneshot, unstructured problem solving.
Duncan and Zaltman (1975)	Questions on the ethics of change.

authors developed classifications which describe the relationship between the manager and the scientist who could be an operations researcher or member of an information services department staff.

Table 2.2 presents the various positions where:
A = manager understands the researcher
B = researcher understands the manager

Table 2.2   Churchman and Schainblatt

	B	B'
A	Mutual understanding	Communication
A'	Persuasion	Separate functionalist

By examining the four cells in the table, one can describe four points of view. In the "separate functionalist" position, the manager does not understand the researcher nor does the researcher understand the manager. This cell separates the functions of management and research; the two never coincide. The "communicator" emphasizes the need for creating more understanding on the part of the manager, and this communications is independent of the personality of the manager. The scientist does not need a detailed understanding of the manager.

The "persuader" examines the manager's personality; the manager does not develop a clear understanding of the scientist. However, the scientist understands enough about the manager to overcome any resistance to his or her recommendations. The "mutual understander" adopts a synthetic approach encompassing the positive aspects of the previous positions. This individual tries to bring about the successful merger of managers and research. The mutual understanding position is very complex, it is not just mutual appreciation, but the scientist learns from the manager and vice versa. There is extensive empathy among the parties.

This paper stimulated sufficient interest that an issue of *Management Science* (vol. 12, no. 2) was devoted to invited responses to the original paper. Empirical studies were also conducted to test the responses of practitioners to this classification scheme. Dykman (1967) administered a questionnaire to a group of managers in a business school program and to operations research professionals. The managers were willing to accept the idea that the fuctions of the scientist and the manager are separate at least in the short run. Both the OR analyst and the manager were in favor of greater understanding.

Managers agreed more with the communicator role while the OR professional agreed more with the persuader. A majority of respondents, however, rejected the separate positions in favor of an approach based more on understanding each other's approach. A follow-up study conducted by Duncan (1974) involved a questionnaire survey of managers who were training for different positions and researcher groups (academicians in a professional society). The two groups rejected the separatist functionalist position and advocated greater mutual understanding. It appears that the separate functionalist approach is not deemed desirable, but there is no consensus on what kind of relationship between the user and designer is best.

Bennis argues in the following issue of *Management Science* that good relations can be produced from building trust and valid communications without recourse to understanding. Dyckman suggests this may be an operational way to arrive at mutual understanding. Churchman and Schainblatt, however, would argue that understanding removes the need for building trust.

Mitroff (1975a) tried to expand on mutual understanding in his study of forty scientists who participated in the Apollo spaceshot missions. The scientists were interviewed four times during the course of the Apollo flight. The study looked at the extent to which the scientist could indentify specific scientists who exhibited at a high degree of prior commitment to hypotheses or theories on the nature of the origin of man. Individuals identified would have a high degree of reluctance to give up their ideas in light of evidence from the moon.

Extreme differences were found among scientists and several patterns emerged. One pattern was formed by scientists who made bold and imaginative theories and expanded from incomplete data. Another group consisted of conservative scientists who relished numbers almost for their own sake and who were often brilliant experimentors.

Mitroff drew implications for implementation and mutual understanding from the study. The highest form of mutual understanding occurs when a scientist responds to the intentions of another scientist. The understanding scientist is also able to give a critical and sympathetic explanation and justification for the psychology of the other scientist that differs from his or her own. The scientist also understands his or her own psychology. Mitroff concludes that "self-reflection is a necessary precondition for the understanding of others" (Schultz and Slevin 1975).

The need for mutual understanding is still debatable. It is certainly necessary for the designer to understand the tasks of the user. However, to what extent should the user understand the designer? The user should probably have some understanding of a system, but how much is needed? Over a decade later, we still have little evidence from which to determine what type of understanding between the user and designer of an information system is desirable or necessary to facilitate implementation.

A Framework for Research

Mason and Mitroff (1973).   The authors have proposed a framework for research on management information systems. They suggest that an information system consists of a *person* of a certain *psychological type* facing a problem in some *organizational context* who needs *evidence* to arrive at a solution. The evidence is made available through some *mode of presentation*.

Mason and Mitroff described the following types of problems: 1) structured (decisions under certainty, risk, and uncertainty); 2) unstructured or wicked decisions.

The framework also describes different methods of generating evidence based on philosophical models, for example, Lockean for evidence based on data or Hegelian for evidence developed by conflicting positions on an issue.

Mason and Mitroff define organizational context using the Anthony classification (see chapter 1) of strategic planning, managerial control and operational control decisions. Finally, the mode of presentation can be personalistic, for example, drama or art, or impersonalistic such as company reports or a computer-based system. The Mason and Mitroff paper is a major contribution to the information systems field. At a time when most research in systems was narrow and technical, this paper called attention to the context of systems, the organization and the widespread individual differences which influence systems design. The paper is strongly recommended to anyone associated with the design of systems.

Situational Normativism

Shakun (1972).   Shakun presents a philosophy of implementation called situational normativism which is a descriptive normative approach to decision-making. A descriptive behavioral model is first constructed which describes the real world decision situation according to the values of the participants (the objectives and goals) and decision rules from the existing system.

Next the implementor constructs a mathematical model of the existing system for normative purposes. The researcher does not view the constraints of the existing system as fixed. The normative solution involves searching for changes in these constraints and a solution satisfying modified constraints. This process represents a search by the manager and the researcher for a "synthesized situational frame of understanding within which solutions to the decision situation can be found."

Shakun argues that situational normativism can relax the cognitive style constraint between the analytic operations researcher and heuristic manager since each is learning from the other. He provides several examples of this approach to implementation.

Situational normativism suggests that contingent factors can act as a constraint on implementation. The analyst probably does not build mathematical models of existing information processing systems as in situational normativism, but he or she does search for ways to eliminate present constraints through the application of new technology.

Process Theories

Zand and Sorensen (1975). These authors present both a process theory and an empirical study to test the theory. The Zand and Sorensen theory is based on Lewin's approach to change which divides the change process into three components: unfreezing, changing, and refreezing.

Unfreezing prepares for a change in behavior. Unfreezing may occur for a computer-based information system by disconfirmation, for example, low levels of performance. Unfreezing could also occur from postitive feedback such as an encouraging remark from a superior as a result of action taken from the output of a system. In the moving state we conceptualize the problem and acquire information on which forces impede change. In making a change it is important to develop alternative solutions and choose a course of action. For information systems design this stage is the development of a new system.

Refreezing occurs through confirmation, psychological support, and confidence. These might come from responses of others, better performance or similar feedback. In a case of information systems hopefully information processing is better than before the system was developed.

Zand and Sorensen derived hypotheses from the Lewin framework which proposed that favorable forces at each stage are positively correlated with successful change and vice versa. These researchers surveyed 391 members of a management science society and received 154 responses. To define the forces the researchers solicited critical incidents from eleven experienced management scientists who described critical change processes, one of which had been very successful, the other extremely unsuccessful. The interview results were subjected to content analysis to find easily identifiable change units with a single meaning.

Seven behavioral scientists classified each of the content units into categories or forces from the Lewin theory and placed the unit into one of several possible levels of favorableness. The criteria of high agreement, salience, and consistency were used to select items for a pilot questionnaire which was pre-tested. The final questionnaires contained 64 items which respondents answered on 5-point scales ranging from 1) statement accurately depicts what occurred, to 5) statement accurately depicts opposite of what occurred. A follow-up questionnaire went to 39 randomly selected subjects through the mail to test reliability.

The results after some further reduction in the number of items on the questionnaire strongly supported the hypotheses in that forces favorable to each phase correlated positively with successful change and vice versa. The authors concluded that unfreezing is a complex and unstable phase. There is a great deal of uncertainty involved, especially when the nature of the problem is not clear.

During the unfreezing stage the parties are also developing a relationship which complicates focusing on the task. Change agents may spend too little time unfreezing, for example, by not seeing that all potential users accept the need for a system. All parties need to recognize the reasons for a change or the information services department staff and the system may become adversaries of users. A superior system helps in refreezing and success and refreezing circularly reinforce each other.

The Zand and Sorensen study was very thorough and the results provide strong support for the Lewin model. This work provides solid evidence for a theory and suggests that a broad process approach (the Lewin model) can be successful in implementation. It is an important piece of research and demonstrates that process theory can be tested in a well-designed study.

Schultz and Slevin (1977). These authors propose a model of the implementation process for OR/MS models based on an adaptive process model by Robertson. The stages in this model are:

1. Problem perception—recognition that the problem exists.
2. Awareness—a solution is proposed and a user becomes aware of action which can be taken to solve the problem.
3. Comprehension—the user learns about the system.
4. Attitude formation—the user becomes favorably or unfavorably predisposed toward the solution.
5. Behavioral intention—the attitudes above and other factors become an intention to use or reject a system.
6. Trial—the user tries the model.
7. Adoption—this means acceptance and continued use of the model.
8. Performance evaluation—the user undertakes an evaluation and audits performance.

Schultz and Slevin arrayed the Robertson stages against explanatory variables in three classes: behavioral, technical, and environmental. The individual variables in these classes have all been studied in factor research.

The Schultz and Slevin model seems more applicable to decision-oriented OR modeling than information systems. Information systems design is a major investment and often involves large numbers of users. However, the general approach of Schultz and Slevin will influence our synthesis in chapter 5. Their contribution has been to combine a process model with factor study results.

Lucas (1974). The author proposes a design philosophy based on user participation and influence. This design approach consists of three major components:

1. User controlled design is the first part of the approach; the user is in charge of the design process. The analyst becomes a catalyst explaining options to the user who makes a

final decision. Design begins with the definition of output and proceeds to system processing logic, file creation and the development of input.

2. The second component is careful attention to the user interface, that is, the part of the system seen by the user. This part of the system often proves frustrating for users, discourages the utilization of the system, and produces high levels of dissatisfaction with it.

3. The final component of the design approach is a definition of systems quality based on user criteria. The author feels too many times systems have been technologically successful, but they have failed in the eyes of users. User control is the key to this approach and the user defines major parts of the system. The resulting product should have a good interface and quality should be automatically based on user criteria.

The authors presents several case studies to show that users can in fact design their own systems. There are, however, several problems that can develop with this approach. First, the analyst may perceive a diminished role and systems will take more elapsed time to develop. The time required for users is extensive and users may feel they are not capable of controlling design.

The Lucas approach is one extreme of those calling for user participation and influence in design. He gives the user almost complete influence over any system, given reasonable cost and technological constraints. The Lucas position at one extreme may help to move designers toward more user influence even if the user is not in control. Lucas also offers suggestions of how to bring about involvement.

Indirect Implementation Strategies

Galbraith (1979). This author has developed an approach to change through a case study of the implementation of computer process control equipment in a manufacturing plan. Computers were placed with new manufacturing equipment desired by the local plant even though they were not necessary. Top management at the local site requested the new equipment and computers as an "add on" were acceptable. This strategy helped place the new technology in the plants.

For protection purposes the new technology was placed in a "management island" and financed by corporate headquarters. After a suitable period of protection the new equipment was diffused into the plant. Several techniques aided this process.

1.   Plant development teams create a local capability in computer technology. This team consists of technical experts from headquarters, local technical staff and operating managers.

2.   Managers are transferred from the "management island" to other areas. They become integrated with the rest of the plant and encourage the adoption of new technology.

Galbraith presents several examples where this approach to implementing new technology is working well. He suggests that the method shows how top management support can be employed by:

1.   Creating   a   climate   in   which   the   problem   is acknowledged.
2.   Providing adequate resources to the user.
3.   Helping establish a solution through the "management island."
4.   Providing financial and psychological support to newly transferred managers.

The technical staff group is also sensitive to the relationships needed to develop linkages within the organization and to develop a broad political base. Galbraith feels the approach is consistent with the Zand and Sorensen and Lewin approaches to change.

Galbraith contributes an example where an indirect implementation approach was successful. He offers an alternative to more direct approaches. This work also points out concrete steps that management can take to encourage implementation.

*Bean and Radnor (1979).** The authors explore the use of intermediaries to link OR/MS personnel to their clients. They examine OR/MS though similar approaches have been employed
in developing information systems, for example, the use of di-
visional analysts, user representatives and other liaison agents.
The idea behind a liaison group is that a buffer can be formed
between highly differentiated units with dissimilar value systems, different time horizons and problem environments.

The Bean and Radnor study began with 18 large industrial
firms and was extended to 43 projects in two firms through the
analysis of critical events. The first type of intermediary studied
was linked functionally to the client, for example, an industrial
engineering group for a production system. The evidence suggests this type of intermediary is more effective in bringing
about successful implementation than are direct exchanges
between OR and client groups. Functionally-oriented intermediaries are also more effective than those who are control-oriented, for example, auditors.

The authors speculate that the use of intermediaries was
beneficial in this study, but may become less necessary as OR
groups become well established in the organization. The idea
of an intermediary is another suggestion of strategies one can
follow in implementation. One similar trend in systems development is the creation of user-analyst positions. Individuals with
a systems background work for users in design and interface
with a systems staff.

Summary

Indirect approaches to implementation are focused on the
highly differentiated attitudes, personal and situational factors
and cognitive style which may exist between the implementor
and the user. The need for user action is often reduced by these
approaches, for example, the direct involvement in the Gal-

* This Northwestern factor study is described here because it differs from other factor
studies.

braith case was limited to the "management island." Particularly, where it is difficult to obtain user involvement or a history of bad experiences exist and users or analysts resist user participation, these indirect mechanisms can facilitate implementation.

OBSERVATIONS

Practice

The authors discussed in this section present recommendations for implementation and insights on the implementation process based on their experience. These suggestions are helpful, but do not really constitute theories.

Malcom (1965). This author proposes that the organization establish a program for operations research/management science. He feels that

1. The implementation phase is not properly planned.
2. A divergence between those interested in theory and practice exist.
3. It is difficult to measure the effectiveness of operations rsearch.
4. Implementation costs are generally understated.

Malcom argues that a firm needs an operations research development plan and should carefully consider where to place the implementation responsibility in the organization. Though Malcom is interested in OR, some of his observations are quite germane to information systems, especially the lack of consideration of implementation, the underestimates of costs and the difficulty of measuring the results of information systems projects.

Ackoff (1967). In his classic article on management misinformation systems Ackoff suggests the following myths of systems development which he feels are common misconceptions in systems analysis and design. Ackoff criticizes the following assumptions:

1. The critical deficiency under which most managers operate is the lack of relevant information.
2. The manager needs the information he wants.
3. If the manager has the information he or she needs, his or her decision making will improve.
4. Better communication between managers improves organizational performance.
5. A manager does not have to understand how the information system works, only how to use it.

Ackoff presents a number of examples which demonstrates how these commonly held myths can be incorrect and lead to difficulties. Clearly his observations are highly relevant for information systems design. It is interesting to note his position on understanding reflects the Churchman and Schainblatt arguments for mutual understanding and Lucas' design approach. Ackoff is also consistent with an approach which emphasizes the user as heavily influential in systems development.

McCoubrey and Sulg (1976). These authors have reported their experiences with operations research at the Converse Rubber Company. Their recommendations can be grouped into the following categories:

1. Develop a problem orientation instead of focusing on techniques.
2. Pay special attention to project selection; do not be afraid to defer or reject a proposal.
3. Concentrate on project organization and control.
4. Observe interpersonal relation and realize that a political jungle exists.
5. Be sure to communicate carefully.
6. Understand the importance of and problems with data.
7. Hire staff with a management orientation.

Many of their recommendations are focused on technical factors in implementation, especially those on data and data bases. They also recognize differences in personal and situational factors and decision support, for example, all their recommendations that users have different value systems and frames of reference. McCoubrey and Sulg offer very practical suggestions based on their considerable experience.

Hammond (1974).   Hammond discusses some of the benefits of management science including the ability to help structure problems, extend information processing abilities, and process data that otherwise might be uncollectable. However, there are serious obstacles to obtaining these benefits, especially in one-shot, unstructured decision problems. Improper expectations about the purpose of analysis and the roles of manager and scientist create problems. Other difficulties are created from strong conceptions about the nature of a problem and its solution. Too often an analyst jumps to an easy solution too quickly.

There may be sharp differences between the characteristics of the management scientist and the decision maker, including different goal orientations, time horizons, experiences, cognitive style, personal styles, problem definition, validation of solution and degree of structure preferred. Hammond argues for a closer support role for the scientist in one-shot, unstructured problems.

Hammond points out differences between the user and the information systems staff and the need to consider user characteristics and the relationship with the analyst as well as the task. While little evidence is presented, the suggestions are appealing.

Ethical Considerations

Duncan and Zaltman (1975).   The authors raise a number of questions about the ethics of the change agent in implementation. These include:

1. The compatability of the change agent consultant and client goals. Misperceptions and hidden motivation often exist instead of honesty; for example, developing information systems as a part of a power struggle in the organization. In other instances, the consultant needs follow on work, etc.
2. The imposition of change agent values. How much freedom do we have to influence the behavior of others? What are the values of the change agent?
3. The selection of the client. Should the information systems specialist design any system requested by the client, even when he or she knows it is not needed?
4. Responsibility for the change. How is the responsibility to be shared? The change agent must participate in problem definition and understand the motivations of the client.
5. The change program. Change often appears less onerous when the attempt to manipulate behavior and tasks is open and honest and potential users participate and are knowledgeable.

The authors developed an ethical value questionnaire, which they administered to the members of the Institute of Management Sciences, obtaining a 43% response rate. There was a substantial agreement among respondents that these questions are significant. The most important issues were discussing conflicts between the goals and the objectives of the change agent and the client. Respondents also felt it important to establish the goals and objectives of the project and determine an implementation strategy openly. Those affected by a new system have the right to be informed about the rationale for solution.

It appears that any design approach which stresses widespread user influence and knowledge of potential users should help resolve these ethical problems. A concern for the relationship as well as the task will lead to the ethical conduct of the change process of systems analysis and design. Note that this research takes on added significance if experiences in

Europe are a precursor of trends in other places. In some European countries, unions and workers must be involved in systems design. These regulations reflect the ethical values suggested by Duncan and Zaltman, especially a position that those affected by a system have certain rights to influence its design.

SUMMARY

All of the theories reviewed in this chapter have a great deal of commonality. They stress understanding the differences among individuals who use a computer-based information system and the different situational and organizational contexts affecting users; they emphasize the relationship between the implementor and the user. Churchman and Schainblatt first raised the issue of understanding between the analyst and user while Mason and Mitroff expand our view of the context in which an information system exists. Zand and Sorensen present both a theory and an empirical test of the theory. Others suggest indirect approaches to implementation or offer suggestions based on experience.

It is safe to conclude that at this stage the field does not really have one complete theory of implementation. Each researcher develops or adopts a theory. However, this work is valuable because it identifies issues and stimulates thought. Theories of implementation must deal with the rich variety of systems, organizations and individual users as well as with the relationships between users and designers.

CHAPTER THREE
FACTOR RESEARCH

THE STUDIES REPORTED in this chapter are primarily concerned with the factors related to implementation success.* These studies were chosen for inclusion in the monograph based on the significance and the quality of research evaluated on the criteria in chapter 1. I have classified these studies into four groups: the general research conducted by the operations research group at Northwestern University, the studies by Lucas, research on decision style, and other factor studies.

THE NORTHWESTERN STUDIES

The studies in this section were conducted at Northwestern University and draw both on practical experience in the development and implementation of OR/MS models and on studies of implementation itself. These multifactor studies were among the first empirical research on implementation. The research is oriented toward operations research, but has many applications for computer-based information systems. Table 3.1 contains a summary of the studies.

* A factor may consist of a single variable or a combination of variables depending on the study. I define a factor as one or a group of related variables in a study.

Table 3.1 The Northwestern Studies

Authors	Year	Study	Factors	General Findings
Rubenstein et al.	1967	Effectiveness of OR groups in 66 company interviews	Management support Client receptivity	Factors appear important in ratings of effectiveness of OR/MS groups and differ in importance by stage of group development
Radnor et al.	1968	Integration of MS groups	Management support Personal, situational factors	Management support important in developing OR/MS groups
Radnor et al.	1970	Implementation Success	Client relations Management support	Good client-researcher relationship and management support are important for successful implementation
Neal and Radnor	1973	Implementation Success	Formal procedures for OR projects	Use of formal procedures, position associated with implementation success
Maher and Rubenstein	1974	Adoption of a model	Adoption, value of output, changes from use	Output quality associated with willingness to adopt, change occurred in communications channel characteristics
Bean et al.	1975	Implementation Success	Structural variables Behavioral variables	Structural and behavioral variables associated with implementation success, few controllable by OR/MS group
Radnor	1979	Implementation Success	Context	Describes variables that influence OR success

Effectiveness of Management Science Groups

Rubenstein et al. (1967).   The researchers published a paper concerning the effectiveness of management science groups in industry. They collected interview data in a cross-sectional field study from 66 industrial firms with captive or internal OR/MS departments. The purpose of the research was to determine factors which significantly affect the introduction, growth and effective performance of OR/MS groups. The authors feel that the stage of the development of the OR/MS group is important. They classify operations research departments as being in a prebirth, introduction, transitional or maturity stage.

The data suggest that the following conditions affect the development of OR groups:

1.   Level of management support

2.   Client receptivity

3.   Organizational and technical competence of the OR/MS group

4.   Organizational location of the group

5.   Influence of the group leader

6.   Reputation of the activity in the organization

7.   Adequacy of resources allocated

8.   Relevance of OR projects to the needs of the organization

9.   Level of opposition in the organization

10.   Prospects for OR/MS success in the organization

These factors differ in importance according to the stage of the development of the group. A mature operations research group can afford an occasional failure without damaging its overall effectiveness while a failure during prebirth might be very serious.

This study encountered difficulties defining effectiveness

and apparently settled on effectiveness as perceived by the interviewees. The authors suggest that the implementation of proposals and programs would be a good indicator of success. While most information services departments are well established, the results of this study present evidence on the importance of management support and the relationship between the client and management scientist. As one of the early factor studies, it stimulated further research. However, it has proven difficult to operationalize the results to suggest how managers can support implementation.

Integration of Management Science

Radnor, Rubenstein, and Bean (1968).   The authors conducted a field study of 66 major firms using interviews to assess the level of integration of OR/MS in the organization. Their paper is primarily descriptive and relates profiles of typical OR/MS personnel and the leadership pattern of OR/MS activities to the integration of the OR/MS function. The personnel needed and the environment for and location of OR/MS activities are also discussed. The authors emphasize the importance of top management support in nurturing this activity. There is preliminary evidence from the study that the use of liaison groups to integrate the operations research specialist and a client has been increasing. While the factor of management support again appears, it is not clear how much of the rest of the study is applicable to the development of information systems.

Implementation

Radnor, Rubenstein, and Tansik (1970).   The researchers developed a rather complex model of the implementation of operations research and R&D in government and private sector organizations and tested the model with data in a cross-sectional field study. From the model they generated a series of propositions which dealt with three major areas:

1. Nature of the client-researcher relationship

2. Level and type of management support for the research activity

3. Type of organization and external environment for the research activity

They tested some of the propositions with the data from interviews in over one hundred government and business organizations. The results indicated that:

1. Relations between the operations researcher and the client are associated with implementation problems and vice versa.

2. Top management support is associated with a low level of implementation problems.

3. There are some indications that a good client relationship is the most important variable.

Client relations really deal with the process of implementation, the topic of the next chapter. This study again points out the role of management support in implementation. It also suggests that relationships are important reinforcing the need to examine the process of implementation. The relationship factor links this research with the process studies in chapter 4.

Formal Procedures and Success

Neal and Radnor (1973).   The study involved the collection of cross-sectional interview data from 178 managers, practitioners, and clients in 108 large business firms. It defined successful implementation precisely as the OR project implementation rate, though several other indicators of success were employed. Major independent variables were whether the OR group had an operating charter or not and the level of procedural elaboration used in pursuing a project.

Interview variables included the OR leader's background, top management involvement and various environmental factors. There was a significant and positive relationship between the existence of a charter and procedural guidelines and the level of implementation success. It appeared that the organizational as opposed to the professional orientation of the OR leader along with top management support were associated with successful implementation.

This finding suggests that the technical specialist needs to develop an organizational identity as well as a professional loyalty. The presence of a charter and guidelines may be an indicator that management is paying attention to the OR activity, something that would tend to encourage others to support OR as well.

Adoption of a Specific Model

Maher and Rubenstein (1974). This study focused on the willingness of users to adopt a specific model. The model in the study is a quantitative approach in the selection of R&D projects based on risk analysis. The model employs a Monte Carlo simulation of various R&D project portfolios and is computer-based. Sixty-four subjects participated in an interview to develop the model and also completed a questionnaire.

Three factors had a strong positive relationship with the potential user's willingness to adopt the experimental model on a routine basis. These were:

1. The perceived value to the individual of data generated by the model

2. The perceived appropriateness of the information input in using the model

3. The perceived value of changes in project research strategy resulting from using the model

The authors also describe changes perceived by the respondents from using the model. These changes include an increased perceived need to develop new communications channels, to increase the use of existing channels, to use new communications channels, and to use existing communications channels more. The value of output was correlated with the perceptions of appropriateness and legitimacy of the input.

The results of this study point out the importance of technical quality, that is, the perceived value of data generated by a computer-based model. The use of such a model can also alter users' behavior, especially with regard to the pattern of communications. However, the strength of the findings were weak and the research model is difficult to follow.

Souder et al. (1975). The willingness of an individual to adopt a model is suggested by Souder as one approach to measuring the implementation success of an R&D project selection model. One can collect data to determine key variables and to estimate a willingness-to-adopt score for an individual to prepare an appropriate implementation strategy. The Souder et al. model was used in three case studies which resulted in the adoption of models and improvements in the subject's willingness to adopt models. In this instance it was possible to increase the probability of successful implementation through the direct intervention of the researchers. This study provides evidence that intervention can influence implementation, an important finding for the implementer.

Structural Variables

Bean et al. (1975). The authors present descriptive material on the development of OR/MS groups and patterns of implementation success. The authors conducted a correlation analysis of cross-sectional data collected from a sample of 108 firms.

Two success variables were defined, percentage of projects completed in the last two or three years being used and a composite index of the OR/MS manager's perceptions of the group's overall success. The authors found that implementation success was linearly correlated with 15 explanatory variables, two of which involved interaction between the OR/MS group and client (percent of leader's time allocated to innovating and to implementing).

Other correlates in the study included structural variables like size of budget and level in the hierarchy of the OR group. Behavioral variables included the orientation of the group leader and top management support. Success scores were based on the OR leader's perceptions, which correlated with many of the variables above. Only six variables appeared on both lists of implementation and perceived success scores and only three of them were subject to direct influence by the OR/MS groups: the six variables were percentage of leader's time allocated to implementation, the formalization of group charter, the quality and availability of data, level in the hierarchy of the management support and top management interest.

While this study points out a large number of potential factors, it seems hard to deal with so many variables. We need to develop some classes of variables which can be considered in planning implementation. It is also interesting to note how few variables were under the influence of the OR/MS goup.

The Context of Implementation

Radnor (1979).   Radnor summarizes much of the Northwestern research and makes a plea to consider the context of OR/MS implementation. He suggests the following dimensions of implementation:

1. OR/MS programs, projects and portfolios

2. OR/MS as a change phenomenon

3. The environment

4. The organization

5. Operations (technology)

6. Management

7. Resources

Radnor discusses the first two dimensions in detail by filling in operational variables in each class, for example, the development of a project profile includes estimating costs and benefits, the scope and extent of project impact, etc. He recommends a similar approach to practitioners as an aid to planning implementation. This paper is a valuable summary and also draws conclusions for action from the studies.

Conclusions

The Northwestern studies include a large number of variables and relationships. Several different models guided this research and the studies focused on OR/MS implementation in a number of organizations and on several insightful case studies. The researchers' primary interest is in operations research and management science, but many of their observations are important for the implementation of computer-based information systems.

These studies are important because they were the first major implementation studies based on data. They have identified a large number of factors, the most consistent of which across the studies are management support and the client-researcher relationship.

We need to move now toward better models to explain the relationship among variables. Also we must consider carefully the similarity between models and information systems in deciding how much to generalize from these findings.

THE LUCAS STUDIES

The studies in this section were undertaken by Lucas; they are generally of individual companies and most of them involve only one system (see table 3.2). The studies all involved computer-based information systems and only one of these systems included an operations research model. The dependent variables which were used to measure implementation success were use of the system where use was voluntary or satisfaction for systems which have to be used. Also, several studies included measures of whether the respondent was likely to take action as a result of some output from an information system.

While these studies were set within single firms, they generally included a large number of respondents making it possible to examine different situational and personal factors and different decision styles. Only differences in environmental variables across the companies must necessarily be omitted from such a research design.

The University Study (1973). This study included users of administrative computer systems at a major university. The information services department staff had developed a number of batch systems for applications such as accounting, payroll, employee records, statistical and administrative records. The results also included data on an experimental on-line system currently being installed; this system served a number of administrative functions.

Users participated in a questionnaire survey which provided data on their attitudes and ratings of computer service: 117 responses were received. Members of the information services department staff also rated the computer systems on criteria of interest to users rather than purely technical criteria.

The findings indicated that user attitudes toward the system were significantly and positively related to ratings of system quality by both users and the information services department staff. The results were even stronger for reported use; user attitudes were strongly and positively related to use as were quality ratings.

Table 3.2 Lucas Studies

Study	Year	Factors	General Findings
University	1973	Attitudes toward system System quality Use	Use positively related to rating of system quality and user attitudes toward systems
Sales force	1975a	Attitudes toward system System quality Decision style Personal and situational variables Use of information system	All independent variables associated with different kinds of use. Favorable attitudes predict use, results hard to forecast for decision style and personal and situational factors
Branch bank	1975a	Decision style Personal and situational variables Likelihood of taking action	Decision style and personal and situational variables related to use of reports and likelihood of taking action
Planning models	1976	Attitudes toward model, model characteristics and support Personal and situational factors Decision style Use Action	Attitude, support, personal and situational factors, decision style, all associated with successful implementation
Brokerage firm OR Model	1979	Attitudes toward model Personal and situational factors Management support Decision style	Personal and situational, decision style associated with attitudes; use; management support and decision style also related to taking action from model
OCR system	1978a	Cost and benefits of use Satisfaction	Satisfaction reduced for group using new OCR system, evidence that benefits not realized and costs too high for user
Medical IS & R	1978c	Management support Use	Management support strongly related to use

The performance of the on-line system had been very erratic and its command language was difficult to use. Comparing the responses of users and the information services department staff showed significantly less favorable attitudes among users of the on-line system compared to users of batch systems. Clearly, users are able to distinguish among systems they use, and this distinction is reflected in attitudes, perceptions and ratings of technical quality. The results offer evidence that attitudes differ depending on the quality of the system encountered.

A Sales Information System (1975a). The company in this study is a major manufacturer of ready-to-wear apparel. Three divisions of the company participated in the study which included a total of 419 sales representatives. Questionnaires were supplemented by data from company records. The system in the research was a sales information application which accepted input from orders completed by sales representatives. The output of the system was a monthly report showing total sales activity on a year-to-day basis for each account assigned to the sales representative. This output contained data for the past twelve months on units shipped, canceled and bookings for the next four months. Sales figures were included on the report with year-to-date and last year-to-date comparisons.

Several different measures of system use were developed from the questionnaire. Analysis of the data showed a strong positive relationship between favorable user attitudes toward the system and its use. Decision-style variables were also associated with some types of use of the output as were a variety of personal and situational factors. However, it was difficult to predict the direction of the association between use and personal and situational factors in advance. Favorable perceptions of output quality were associated with higher levels of system use for the vast majority of users. The results support the existence of a relationship among attitudes, situational and personal variables, decision style and system use, a measure of implementation success.

A Bank Information System (1975a). This cross-sectional

study was conducted in a major California Bank with well over 200 branches. Each branch has a manager and an assistant manager plus an operations staff. The manager is responsible for the branch; he or she reports to division management. Officers have loan limits, but there is latitude for negotiations on terms and conditions.

Branch data were collected from a computer-based performance system, which reported on five indicators. Demographic data from the management science department of the bank were also used to predict performance not under the control of the branch manager. This component was removed statistically from branch performance to arrive at an estimate of the performance of the branch based on management actions.

Branch managers and assistant managers provided usage data for four major reports where use was discretionary through a questionnaire returned by 316 respondents (a 95 percent response rate). Data analysis included predictions of use, users' perceptions of output quality, personal and situational variables, decision style and performance for the four reports.

The results were strongest for decision style variables; different management approaches were associated with different report usage patterns. For example, activist managers were the least likely to use reports from the computer system. Personal and situational factors were also very important in predicting use, but again forecasting the direction of the relationship in advance was difficult. As an example, the use of reports was negatively related to education. Age was associated with the likelihood of taking action from the reports, another indicator of successful implementation showing the usefulness of information on the report.

This study is consistent with the results of the prior research. However the difficulty of predicting outcomes based on decision style and personal and situational variables is discouraging. Such independent variables will be of less help in planning for implementation if we are unable to predict their impact.

Planning Models (1976).   The research above deals with large information systems; this study of planning models is for much smaller applications. The models were all developed using a proprietary language on one of two identical time-sharing computers.

Interviews and questionnaires furnished data from 25 planning managers and 16 technical support staff members in a total of 21 companies. The planning models were used for a variety of purposes, most of which were taking immediate action on operational control or managerial control problems. Only four of the models were used for strategic planning purposes.

The results showed strong associations among the technical characteristics of the model, management support and involvement, situational and personal factors and user attitudes toward the model. Implementation was measured by several usage indicators including data from the time-sharing service bureaus where the models were run and self-report measures from the questionnaire. Action taken based on the model was also included as a measure of implementation success. Successful implementation was strongly associated with planning model characteristics, positive attitudes, personal and situational factors, decision style and management support.

For decision style the opposite of the prediction that more technically oriented managers would be more likely to use the model was found. Instead, less technically oriented managers reported more use of the model. One possible explanation is that more technically oriented managers are aware of the shortcomings and assumptions of a model and are less willing to rely on it. This finding highlights the importance of decision style and the complexity of its relationship with implementation success.

A Brokerage Model (1979). The company involved in this study is a major brokerage firm with offices throughout the United States. Account executives buy and sell securities for customers of the firm on a commission basis. These individuals have radically different approaches to their job; some conduct extensive research while others concentrate on sales. The firm has a division which provides research information for the account executive and for customers.

The company had developed a large operations research model to recommend investment strategies. The model was proprietary and was based on exponential smoothing and forecasting techniques. The model used technical analysis which involves an explanation of the structural aspects of the market rather than the characteristics of any individual company. A fundamental analysis instead would rely on the firm and consider variables like the company, markets and products, quality of management etc.

The output of this operations research model was recommended industry groups for purchase or sale. The model staff at company headquarters suggested specific securities and the firm distributed these recommendations and the model output to all branches each week.

The account executive could use the output of the model to recommend specific securities or industries, as a timing device when to enter or leave the market or as a sales tool to attract customers.

Data for this cross-sectional study were collected from 423 sales representatives and account executives (a 90 percent response) who completed questionnaires, and from company records.

The decision style of account executives was significantly related to attitudes towards the OR model and attitudes in turn were good predictors of model use. Decision style and situational and personal factors were also related to use, for example, having a large number of institutional accounts was associated with high levels of model use.

Examining the reaction across major geographical divisions in the company also showed marked differences in usage. Some of these differences were undoubtedly related to the extensive efforts by the headquarters staff to increase the visibility and use of the model in one division. Office manager support and decision style were also related to likelihood of taking action based on the output of the model.

This study is significant because it was possible to include a large number of respondents who had the opportunity to use the same OR model presented as an information system. Use was entirely voluntary. Because of the differing levels of use associated with the model we have evidence that there are variables which affect implementation beyond strictly technical factors. The same identical system experienced varying levels of use for organizational and behavioral reasons.

An OCR System (1978a). The OCR study was conducted among sales representatives of the same apparel firm described earlier, but at a point much later in time than the earlier study. The firm was introducing an experimental optical character recognition (OCR) order entry form in one division; this new application also included new computer programs for processing orders.

Data in this longitudinal field study were collected at two points in time through a questionnaire. The instrument was administered to an experimental division where the new form was introduced and a random sample in a comparable control group in a similar division not using the new OCR form. A total of 114 sales representatives from an original group of approximately 190 completed both questionnaires, 56 in the experimental group and 58 in the control group.

The questionnaire included items on the benefits of the system, the personal costs of using the system and the satisfaction of sales representatives. The results showed that the perceived quality of service actually declined due to the startup problems and experimental nature of the new computer system. Sales representative satisfaction dropped in both divisions, but it dropped significantly more in the experimental group using the new OCR form.

A cross-lagged correlation analysis indicated that during the time of the introduction for the new OCR system, service quality became more strongly related to sales representative satisfaction. The data support an interpretation that the costs of use of the new system exceeded the benefits to the sales representative resulting in lower levels of satisfaction. The problem of implementation costs and benefits to individuals is very important and will be discussed further. The evidence from this study is significant because of the longitudinal research design and control group.

A Medical Information Storage and Retrieval System (1978c). A major pharmaceuticals firm developed an on-line information storage and retrieval system for medical research using CRT's for browsing and retrieval. Hard copies of articles were kept in file cabinets and only abstracts in the computer data base were displayed on line in response to user requests (Lucas 1978c).

The system could be used by scientists to aid their research through the retrieval of general bibliographies or specific topics and authors. The system could be used directly or through a library or research assistant. A monitor built into the on-line system traced usage; 180 medical researchers out of 205 surveyed completed questionnaires on their use of and attitudes toward the system.

Respondents were asked to indicate on the questionnaire the names of three people to whom they would turn when first looking for a reference. This reference leader, as it turned out, was generally a manager and more senior person in the laboratory. The respondents were divided into two groups depending on whether they had been chosen as a reference leader or not. Then the group of researchers that was not chosen as references was divided into subgroups depending on the attitudes of its reference leader toward the system, either favorable or unfavorable.

The non-chosen group whose reference leaders had more favorable attitudes was much more likely to have used the information storage and retrieval system and to have favorable attitudes toward it. Non-reference researchers whose reference leader had unfavorable attitudes were not likely to have used the new system at all. These results offer strong evidence of the importance of management support and leadership in encouraging use and implementation.

Summary

The Lucas studies present a rather consistent set of findings, though this may be a function of researcher bias. The studies are based on a simple factor model of implementation and offer guidelines for action. The findings support the importance of technical quality, management support, user attitudes, decision style and personal and situational variables in implementation. Also where these studies overlap with the Northwestern research, the results are consistent.

DECISION STYLE RESEARCH STUDIES

The studies above deal with the relationship of a large number of independent variables and several measures of implementation success. In this section we review studies which examine one individual variable—decision style. Decision style was defined broadly in the Lucas studies as different characteristic ways of approaching a problem. In this section, the researchers make a more precise definition, for example, cognitive style as suggested by Mason and Mitroff. Several different tests have been employed in the following research to classify individuals on how they tend to make decisions. We shall group all of these studies into a factor call "decision style." The studies below were primarily conducted in the laboratory which increases control over extraneous variables. See table 3.3 for a summary of the studies to be discussed in this section.

Cognitive Style

Huysmans (1970). Huysmans conducted research in a laboratory setting to determine the possible constraints of cognitive style on the adoption of operations research recommendations. Experimental subjects played the president of a simulated firm and the roles of four other managers were simulated in the ex-

Table 3.3 Decision Style Studies

Author	Study	Year	General Findings
Huysmans	Experiment	1970	Cognitive style can act as an implementation constraint
Doktor and Hamilton	Experiment	1973	Cognitive style and subject population differences affect acceptance of management science recommendations
Larreche	Experiment	1979	Integrative complexity is associated with the extent and efficiency of information search behavior using marketing models
Kilmann and Mitroff	Experiment	1976	Individuals with different cognitive styles have different ideal organizations corresponding to these styles
Mitroff, Nelson, and Mason	Experiment	1974	An information system can affect cognitive style especially the preference for learning about both sides of a problem

periment. Subjects were classified as analytical or heuristic in reasoning for different experimental treatments. Analytical reasoning reduces problems to a core of underlying causal relationships. An explanation is often facilitated by a model for an analytic decision maker. The heuristic reasoner emphasizes workable problem solutions for the total problem situation; this decision maker looks for analogous problems in searching for a solution.

Two experimental treatments were given managers who were classified as either analytic or heuristic. The subjects had to adopt or reject an operations research recommendation related to marketing and production decisions. The researchers also analyzed messages sent by subjects as either organizational (to establish responsibility or authority) or functional (related to solving a problem).

The accounting manager who was simulated followed two approaches: explicit understanding or integral understanding for an operations research model. The explicit understanding report included actual formulas while the integral understanding form did not. The experimenter tested three hypothesis through 35 experiments.

Heuristic subjects rejected the recommendation of the accounting manager when he presented the technical analysis. Analytics responded more positively if the explicit understanding approach was used. Most of the heuristics and analytics receiving the integral understanding approach had a high degree of adoption and these individuals had a higher degree of adoption than the heuristics receiving the explicit understanding approach. The author concluded that cognitive style can operate as a constraint on implementation. He suggests that operation researchers should take cognitive style into account and realize that when the orientation of the manager and researcher do not agree, the manager may reject the researcher or the source of information.

Huysmans first pointed out the possible problems created by cognitive style in implementation. While this study was complex, it was conducted in a well-controlled environment. More than any other research, the importance of cognitive style was established by this study.

Doktor and Hamilton (1973).   These two authors also studied cognitive style and the acceptance of management science recommendations through an experiment employing graduate students and production managers. The Churchman and Shainblatt model discussed earlier provided the background for this experiment.

There were three identical sessions in the experiment. The researchers at first administered a cognitive style test and then the subjects were asked to read a simple business case and assume the role of a top manager. The subjects received one of two versions of a consultant's report (depending on their score on a cognitive style test, with report alternatives based on ranks on the test). The subject recorded on a questionnaire whether or not he or she would accept the report. One consultant's report was analytical and included formulas in the body of the report while the other report was general, and the formulas were contained in an appendix.

For fifty students, the low analytic subjects were more likely to accept the report than high analytic subjects regardless of which report was received. Low analytics had a greater tendency to accept analytic reports while high analytics tended to accept the general report over the analytic report.

There was little difference among acceptances of recommendations by managers regardless of their cognitive style. However, students who were low analytics had cognitive style scores which were almost as high as high analytic managers. The researcher matched students and managers based on test scores and analyzed the students. The matched students showed a greater propensity to accept the report than the managers.

Cognitive style, differences in two subject populations and personal and situational factors were related to the acceptance of management science recommendations in this experiment. However, the results were not as originally hypothesized, a common problem with cognitive style research.

Other Decision Style Studies

Larreche (1979). This researcher looked at a slightly different aspect of decision style called cognitive complexity. This theory is based on work by Schroeder, Driver, and Streufert and suggests that individuals tend to process information at different levels of integration. Low integration structures are characteristic of individuals who integrate the problem dimensions perceived in a fixed or hierarchical fashion which is absolute. High levels of integration correspond to the decision maker who considers alternative combinations of dimensions and generates complex relationships among variables.

Integrative complexity combines with information complexity to determine a level of individual information processing. Information complexity consists of the information load, diversity and rate of change of information. Noxity is the severity of adverse consequences from an outcome and eucity is the amount of reward received.

Larreche tested two hypotheses about information processing related to marketing models using 24 MBA students. Students ran two marketing models: one involving regression analyses and the other competitive bidding. Access to the models was measured by a time-sharing computer on which the students also took a cognitive complexity test. For the first model more integratively complex individuals searched for more information and exhibited more efficient search behavior. The same pattern held, though less strongly, for model two.

Subjects generally rated the first model more highly on response time, output and educational value. The author suggests that this evidence provides support for the idea that differences in integrative complexity and information search behavior are impacted more by models which generate levels of environmental complexity closer to the optimum level for the user.

Kilmann and Mitroff (1976).   This study by Kilmann and Mitroff offers interesting evidence for the importance of cognitive style as a key variable in determining the actions of the decision maker. Participants in an executive program completed a cognitive style test, which classified them according to a Jungian framework of sensing-thinking, sensing-feeling, intuitive-thinking and intuitive feeling. Each participant was then asked to write an essay describing his or her ideal organization.

The ST (sensation-thinking) type emphasized precision, control, specificity, impersonal analysis and logical and orderly reasoning; the ST likes quantitative analysis. The ideal organization of the ST's was characterized by an extreme emphasis and concentration on specifics and factual details. ST types were very sensitive to the physical features of their work environment; in their ideal organization everyone knew exactly what his or her job was. There was no uncertainty as to what was expected; the emphasis was on work and work roles, not on the individuals to fill the jobs.

The NT (intuitive-thinking) type stressed conceptual analysis as opposed to precision and quantification. This individual finds that variables cannot be specified sufficiently for quantification. The NT reasons qualitatively and strives toward impersonal objectivity; he or she tends to specify variables and their interrelationships, if only in a conceptual and verbal manner. The ideal organization of the NT's emphasized broad, global issues; these individuals omitted almost any detailed facts. The NT's focused on general concepts and issues, not on detailed work rules or lines of authority. They were concerned with ill-defined, macro-economic issues like equitable wages for all. The NT is impersonal as is the ST, but the NT focused on concepts and theories of organization while, for the ST, individuals exist to serve the organization.

Both the SF (sensing-feeling) and NF (intuitive-feeling) relied on subjective and value laden criteria for analysis rather than logic and principles. The major difference between SF and NF is that the former type strives for some precision while the latter is abstract and loosely defined in his or her approach to problems. It is interesting to note that the NF is completely the opposite of the ST. These two types actually oppose one another since they are based on different and conflicting preferences for information and decision making styles. According to Kilmann and Mitroff, the ST approach has dominated management science efforts to date.

The ideal organization for the NF's showed an absence of theory; these types were concerned with the detailed human relations in their organizations. Unlike the ST's who were concerned with work roles, the SF's were concerned with the human qualities of the specific people who fill the roles. The NF, on the other hand, did not want to get down to specifics; he or she was interested in the general theory of organizations and on the personal and human goals of organizations. The NF was concerned for example, with serving humanity; the organization exists to serve the personal and social needs of people.

This experiment shows some of the important differences among individuals with different cognitive styles. If one believes that different styles exist in an organization where an information system is to be implemented, then decision style is an important variable in the design process.

Mitroff, Nelson, and Mason (1974). This study of mythological information systems reversed the direction of causality in the relationship between use and decision style. We have been discussing decision style as a constraint on implementation, but in this research the authors used an information system to change decision style. In the experiment 30 subjects played a game called "beat the computer." In this game the subject chose the row of a matrix which would give the highest payoff. The computer randomly chose the column and the subject received the score at the intersection of the row he chose and the column chosen by the computer.

Two experts programmed on the computer presented a dialogue describing their positions and recommending a choice to the subject during the experiment. One called Smiley used a max-max or optimistic game strategy and the other called Grumpy used a max-min or pessimistic strategy. Each expert's score was displayed along with the score of the subject. The subjects tended to choose the middle of the conflicting opinions, however, they lost completely if they followed either expert strategy exclusively. After the first round of the experiment a new character emerged named Synthetic Sarah. On the next round she gave advice along with the other two experts and if the subjects followed her recommendations, they won.

The subjects then played Freud, an exercise which explained one-way and two sided personalities. The subject was asked to answer questions designed to elicit attitudes about dialectical thinking. The computer attacked positions which were not two-way and reinforced the respondent who provided two-way answers. The subjects in the experiment showed statistically significant shifts toward more dialectical thinking as measured by a questionnaire as a result of the experiment.

This experiment shows that with effort, decision style may be altered. Clearly there are moral and ethical dimensions to attempting changes in decision style. We shall offer guidelines in chapter 5 for changes which stress open and full communications. The other studies reviewed in this section show that decision style can act as an implementation constraint while the Mitroff et al paper shows that decision style is susceptible to influence under certain conditions.

OTHER FACTOR STUDIES

Research in this section is difficult to classify, though in general these studies have examined general and specific factors related to implementation success. See table 3.4 for a summary.

An Attitudinal Study

Schultz and Slevin (1975).   This study reports a pretest on attitudes and implementation success. These researchers collected data on possible attitudinal variables and developed Likert and semantic differential tests from them. The instruments were pretested on 136 MBA students who responded to questions on their attitudes and intended use of a forecast from a marketing model in a business case. The authors' factor analyzed the attitude items, which yielded good results for the Likert questionnaire. Seven factors and a global score were computed from this instrument. The factors included performance, interpersonal relations, changes, goals, support for the model, client researcher interface and urgency of results.

These factors correlate well with five measures of the likelihood that the respondent would use the model. The factors also correlate with success and the accuracy of the forecast. The researchers conclude that the benefits from the model, management support, and good relationships between the client and researcher are important in implementation. Here, attitudes were strongly associated with implementation success.

A Retrieval System

Swanson (1974).   This study examines the use of a computer-based retrieval system for the management of engineering pro-

Table 3.4 Other Factor Studies

Author	Study	Year	Factors	General Findings
Schultz and Slevin	Attitude	1975	Management support Client-researcher relationship Benefit to client Goal congruence Success	Developed instruments to measure attitudes; factors in general were positively correlated with measures of successful implementation
Swanson	Computer-based retrieval system	1974	Attitudes Involvement Use	Involvement and favorable attitudes associated with a high level of information systems use
Argyris	MS/OR group	1971	Rationality Interpersonal relations	Introduction of information system requires knowledge of the emotional aspects of the organization
Harvey	Project success	1970	Management support Management Science team Problem characteristics Success	Factors related to successful implementation; major variable is management's faith that the effort would solve the problem
Bean and Shewe	Marketing information systems	1976	Attitudes Personal and situational factors Use	Attitudes not as strong a predictor of use as personal and situational factors

jects. One file contains work and project activity data for the most recent 13 weeks at the level of individual group member. The system also features an 18-month summary file of work and activity at the departmental level. The user can generate a large number of personalized reports from this system.

One important variable was the use of the system measured by actual inquiries. *A priori* involvement in design was measured by the frequency with which the manager made requests for changes in the design or the operational state of the system. MIS appreciation was defined by a group of attitudes which were measured using a questionnaire. The author notes that relatively low levels of *a priori* involvement were reported by the managers.

Data from 37 managers indicate that *a priori* involvement is associated with favorable attitudes and favorable attitudes are associated with a high level of use. Further analysis suggests that *a priori* involvement is associated with attitudes and with actual use. The data support a model in which attitudes are an intervening variable between *a priori* involvement and actual use. The author suggests that *a priori* involvement and actual use co-produce favorable attitudes and in turn are co-produced by favorable attitudes.

The Swanson results strongly support the existence of a link between favorable attitudes and use. This study also supports with actual data the importance of user involvement in design. The research seems well-designed and the results credible.

An OR/MS Group

Argyris (1971). Argyris conducted a study of an OR/MS group in a company. There were 20 individuals on the operations research staff. All of the team members were interviewed along with the supervisors above the group leader and meetings and work sessions were tape recorded.

Argyris feels that information systems increase the rationality of management and this creates resistance to their use. The author is concerned with management information systems for top managers, not transactions-oriented systems.

According to Argyris, the problem from these systems include:

1. A reduction of free movement—what was hidden is now open

2. Psychological failure and double bind—systems automate too much of the user's activities, for example, by defining the manager's goals for him or her

3. Leadership based more on competence than power

4. Decreasing feelings of essentiality—rationalization means less need for control of the organization and also for "turning things around"

5. Reduction of politics—departments must learn to cooperate with each other because of information processing

6. New requirements for conceptual thinking—more sophisticated information systems place new demands on users

According to Argyris all of these trends suggest greater rationality which will create stress for users in the organization. If the information system were used effectively, it would free the manager rather than restrict him or her. Argyris argues that the norms and the approach of MIS experts means that stress rather than freedom will result from information systems.

Analysis of the tapes from the study showed that behavior that facilitates or directly inhibits others' behavior and feelings was rarely expressed. The norms for openness to new ideas, risk taking and expressive feelings were very weak. Few feelings of any kind were exhibited in group sessions. Under stress the OR/MS team became much more conforming to ideas and antagonistic feelings were suppressed. Past research showed that top managers also act this way under stress. Both groups then react to the stress in ways that inhibit effective problem solving.

As a solution Argyris calls for more emphasis on interpersonal relations and recognition that emotional problems occur in the organization. Argyris contends that the introduction of information technology is an emotional problem that requires knowledge about the human aspects of the organization, such as personal, small group and organizational norms.

Argyris' work is highly controversial. This study presents data, but they are unusual and hard to assess. Argyris does point out that there is an emotional side to individuals and that individual behavior is likely to affect implementation success.

Model Building

Harvey (1970). Harvey examined factors related to implementation success and failure in helping clients to build models. This consultant cited key variables contrasting successful versus unsuccessful model implementation. The results indicated that characteristics of management, the nature of the problem and the characteristic of the management science team were important in determining implementation success. One of the strongest results was a relationship between success and the belief by management that management science is likely to solve the problem under study.

A Different View of Attitudes

Bean and Shewe (1976). This study presents the results of two studies which they feel disconfirm the existence of a relationship between attitudes and model use. These studies were conducted in 1969 and 1971 and focused on implementation of integrated information systems including several OR models for planning and marketing. The first study used a semantic differential test to measure attitudes which were the independent variables. The dependent variables were used as monitored by the system. There were 65 participants in the study as a part of an in-house training experience.

The authors found a negative relationship between attitudes and use. One explanation offered was that training seemed to raise expectations, which were not met by the system. Another explanation for the negative findings appeared when examining the attitude measures. The items tested represent rather general attitudes toward planning, mathematics, operations research, the general work environment, and management science in general. Research reviewed earlier in the chapter, on the other hand, included attitudes specific to an information system, not attitudes as general as the ones in this study. In discussing a link between attitudes and use of systems, these other studies stressed the importance of attitudes toward the specific system under study.

The second study was retrospective and defined satisfaction using ten attitude items on the consequences of using an information system. Some 38 users completed a questionnaire in two organizations (many from the same group in the first study). Regression analysis was employed to analyze the data. In this study exogenous (personal and situational variables) were significant predictors of views and attitudes were not. However, such a finding does not contradict the existence of a relationship between attitudes and use. It indicates that in this situation using retrospective questions, situational and personal variables proved more important than attitudes in predicting use.

SUMMARY

The factor studies are impressive in scope and number of variables identified. However, this large number of variables is a weakness, too. How can we cope with these numerous factors?

It seems unlikely that any one implementation project could include or even measure all of them.

We can group the variables into larger categories, however, From the results of the research, the following five classes seem to include most of the individual factors:

Technical system quality

Client actions

Attitudes

Decision style

Personal and situational variables

The Northwestern studies suggest the importance of client actions in the form of management support. The Lucas studies provide evidence on the importance of all these classes of variables in implementation; however his findings on decision style were confusing. Huysmans, Doktor, and Hamilton and Mitroff et al., however, provide evidence on the significance of decision style in implementation. Finally, Swanson added weight to the relationship between attitudes and use.

Future factor studies should include more testing of hypotheses derived from models of the implementation process. We have identified many factors through surveys. Now we need to understand what factors are the most important and how they are related to each other.

The major missing consideration from the factor studies is the process of design, though this topic is occasionally included under the category of client-researcher relations. The next chapter examines this variable further as we review process studies of implementation.

CHAPTER FOUR

PROCESS STUDIES

THE RESEARCH IN this chapter is primarily concerned with the process of implementation. The projects included here are generally case studies though some of the cases included survey research. Instead of factors alone, this research tries to explain the relationship among variables with simple, descriptive models of the implementation process.

Process studies usually examine the relationship of the designer and user as a system is developed. The studies frequently identify different stages in the task of developing a system and may suggest how the user-designer relationship should progress as the system moves through the different stages.

There are a number of important issues to consider about the process of design. We should be concerned about some of the following themes:

1. What is the impact of a system on the organization's structure, work groups, and individuals?
2. How do we control the design process (control can be vested entirely in the design team or it can be shared with users)?
3. How does one terminate the relationship between users and the designer so that psychological ownership of the system rests with users?

4. How do we motivate users to accept a new system?
5. What and how can the analyst and user learn from each other?

The studies discussed in this chapter are summarized in table 4.1.

Table 4.1   Process Studies

Author	Study	Year	Process & Stages
Mann and Williams	Electric utility	1960	Entire implementation process for new computer-based system
Mumford and Banks	British banks	1966–1968	Analysis of entire implementation effort with emphasis on planning the potential impact on each individual
Mumford and Henshall	Rolls Royce	1979	The socio-technical approach to participative design
Bjorn-Anderson and Hedberg	Banks	1977	Case studies of bank systems and recommendations for achieving more user involvement
Lucas and Plimpton	Farm workers	1972	Stages in the Kolb–Frohman model
Ginzberg	Multiple projects	1979	Stages in the Kolb–Frohman model for 29 projects
Ginsberg and Ramsey	A bank	1975	Field-centered evaluation and implementation
Vertinsky, Barth, and Mitchell	Multiple companies	1975	Implementation as social change process. Motivation and costs/benefits of change
Narasimhan and Schroeder	Eight case studies	1979	Implementation is a staged process in which management science intervention is the primary force and organizations are significant, indirect forces for change
Boland	Experiment	1976	Interactive vs. interrogative interviews during requirements analysis
Manley	Case study in the Air Force	1979	The use of "strawmen" in several iterations to form a social point for attitude change.

EARLY STUDIES

Mann and Williams (1960).   One of the first studies of the implementation of a computer system is an in-depth case of an electric utility. This paper produced many insights into the implementation process and the impact of computers on the organization. The study focused on an electric utility in the Midwest with over one million customers. The utilty had two accounting divisions, one of which was concerned with bills and records and the other with customer contact on questions of service and payment. There were 800 employees in a central office and 1500 in geographical offices. The new system represented the first attempt at computer-based processing in the utility. The system was designed to maintain customer accounts; the previous system had been on electric tabulating equipment.

Mann and Williams identified a series of stages in the change process:

1. Stability and equilibrium before the change
2. Preliminary planning
3. Detailed preparation
4. Installation and testing
5. Conversion
6. Stabilization
7. New equilibrium after the change

The change was announced in October 1953 and the computer arrived three years later. Conversion began in January 1957 and by 1958 the initial perturbations had smoothed and permanent work assignments were established.

The utility saw the development of the new system as an excuse to review the organization. Management undertook a very broad rethinking of the structure of the organization. The only difficulty with this approach is that the information system may have been perceived as the causal agent behind unsettling organizational changes. One of these changes was the movement of bookkeeping functions from the district to the central office. Customer contact was to be centralized in the sales area;

for example, the meter reading function was moved from accounting to sales.

The authors felt that the participative management style in the accounting division helped it to respond well to changes. On the other hand, the sales department delegated the information systems planning activity to lower levels in the organization and it encountered more implementation difficulty.

The organization decided to make all job grades temporary based on the lack of knowledge as to what final positions would entail. This decision created a great deal of uncertainty for the work force, though almost all employees expected an upgrading of jobs and higher pay to result from the computer system.

The conversion process itself placed heavy time demands on everyone in the company, particularly supervisors. Supervisors needed a mix of technical, human relations and supervisory skills. Some supervisors who were successful in one of these roles had extreme difficulty handling problems in other areas. The authors also felt that the sales department had more trouble adjusting because it was less involved in developing the system and the computer was controlled by accounting. Communications problems arose between sales and accounting. There was limited sharing of information within sales and the sales department described accounting as being unconcerned about customers; they only worried about records and lower costs.

There was general mistrust of the information produced by the system. Some individuals kept old records manually rather than relying on the computer system. There were a large number of errors in the system and there were difficulties in having them corrected. The situation reached the point where a consulting firm was called in to examine the errors. The consulting report indicated that the number of errors was not unusual for this type of system and the presentation of the report forced the sales department and accounting to work together to resolve these problems.

The process of developing final job assignments after the system had been installed proved very difficult. A complicated procedure was used where by the highest level job was filled first and then lower grade positions were assigned. Supervisors tried to find best fit assignments, though this was very difficult to resolve because no supervisor wanted to take anyone but the best candidates. Lower than expected job grades resulted from the change and higher levels of pay were not realized.

The authors concluded from their study that the computer system accelerated the level of formalization and appeared to reduce the status of some decision makers. There was less autonomy for individuals and work groups and there were more deadlines. Greater dependencies were created and there was a need for more coordination. There appeared to be a shift toward centralization contrary to management goals. Many of the jobs replaced were routine and tedious and there was an increase in EDP related jobs. The authors felt that there was some job enlargement. Certainly, there was a greater identification of errors and more responsibility for employees; the unsuccessful worker was very much in the spotlight.

The Mann and Williams paper provides a number of findings on the impact of a system, however, there really was no framework for analysis. The authors did not have a general process model in mind, but instead described stages that were unique to this company. Some of their findings on the impact of computers on the workforce are probably generalizable to other situations.

Mumford and Banks (1967). Mumford and Banks conducted an extensive case study of the installation of computers in two English banks. The computer was an early model and a change occurred over a several year period. Through interviews and questionnaires the researchers studies the reaction of individuals and the impact of the computer system. Before the change few employees were concerned about it. After the installation of the system men were more worried than women over the potential of the computer and its impact on careers. Older individuals of both sexes appeared to have more concerns about job security as a result of the computer system.

Mumford and Banks tried to construct a profile of the chronic change resistor in the organization. They concluded that the most trusted and respected employees of the bank were likely to be the largest resistors of change. Also, older male employees near retirement appeared the most likely to resist change, while younger female clerks were least concerned with the computer system, because at that time, they did not expect to have a long career in the bank. The individuals who were most worried could progress in the organization and identify with the bank's goals; the computer was a threat to their advancement.

In a subsequent book Mumford and Ward (1968) draw upon the bank and other experiences to present an approach to planning for the installation of a computer system. In the appendix of the book they provide an example of a particularly useful approach to planning for change. Mumford and Ward suggest analyzing the probable impact of a system on each potential user prior to installation. The analyst lists the costs and benefits for each individual and tries to plan for conversion accordingly. If the costs are too high the system can be changed or restructured to increase benefits so individuals are encouraged to accept and work with the system.

PARTICIPATIVE APPROACHES

The Sociotechnical Approach

Mumford's early work has progressed to apply the ideas of the sociotechnical method of organizational change to systems design. The sociotechnical method first arose when researchers at the Tavistock Institute studied the failure of engineering changes to improve productivity in coal mining and textile production. These researchers concluded that in addition to a technical system, there was a social system primarily based on the work group which was important in bringing about change. The change agent could not focus on the technical process alone;

instead the change effort had to consider the socio-technical system.

Mumford and her colleagues have stressed participation in systems analysis and design which is a major part of their approach. She identifies three positions on a continuum of user participation in design:

1. The consultative approach leaves most of the decisions on how a system will be designed to a traditional systems design group, though there is a great deal of consultation and discussion with the users at every level.

2. Representative participation means that there is a higher level of participation from a user group. Now the design team for a new system includes representatives of the user department. The value system underlying this approach is that no one has the right to design a job for someone else. According to Davis at UCLA, the role of the expert is to help a worker design his own job.

3. In consensus participation all staff in a user department are involved in systems design throughout the development process. A design group of representatives is elected to join the design team. This group of representatives must obtain feedback and interact with all others in the user department.

Mumford and Henshall (1979).   The authors have written about the application of the third method, consensus democracy, to the design of an information system. The case study took place in the accounts payable and invoice departments of the Rolls-Royce Engine company in England. A batch system existed at the time of the change; a new on-line featuring CRTs was to be developed. Mumford acted as a consultant as the firm wished to redesign jobs at the same time and felt that external expertise was needed.

A formal agreement was reached among all parties at the

beginning of the project; a steering group consisting of the senior managers, the company medical officer and a trades union official along with Mumford was formed.

The book describes in detail the process by which the system was designed and the problems encountered during its development. It is an excellent case study and shows the reader how one might apply the sociotechnical approach to systems design.

In their conclusions, Mumford and Henshall emphasize that the user and analyst will learn in applying this approach. The user learns about work design and systems and the analyst learns how to let users control more of the design process.

In addition to a description, the book contains examples of questionnaires used in planning the change and an example of variance analysis, a key component of sociotechnical change. The first analysis task in developing an understanding of the work system is to identify unit operations. Unit operations are sets of tasks which logically fit together in some way, like the processing of a customer invoice. The unit operations should be integrated and separated from other sets of tasks by some change in the state of the input being processed.

A variance in some weaknesses in the sysem, a portion of the system which can deviate from some desired standard. The variances are listed and placed in a variance matrix. If a variance affects other variances, it is so indicated in the matrix intersection of the row and column entries for the variances involved.

Variance control involves studying the key variances to find out where they originate, where variances are observed and controlled, who is responsible, what is done, what information is required, and possible alternative control mechanisms.

The sociotechnical approach is quite popular in Europe, but its use has not been reported extensively in the literature in the United States. The focus of the sociotechnical approach is on job design and it appears to be most applicable to transactions-oriented systems where there are mainly clerical users. It is not clear that the same approach or same tools of variance analysis are applicable to systems which really provide information like planning systems. However, one can learn a great deal about a well-organized approach to participative design from the sociotechnical approach.

Scandinavian Bank Case Study

Bjorn-Anderson and Hedberg (1977). The authors have reported on a study they conducted of the development of on-line systems in two Scandinavian banks (1977). The research team collected data about the design process and the consequences of the new information systems in interviews with 90 managers, clerks, and members of the design team; 48 members of the design team also completed questionnaires. The authors reported that user satisfaction with the new systems reflected that work roles changed only modestly when dire consequences had been expected. However, the new technology caused unintended changes in work roles and organizational structures in branch offices and between branches and headquarters. The design team gave little consideration to how the information systems could result in an overall improvement in the organization.

The authors' felt that the design teams had focused too extensively on the technology. There were a number of constraints on the designers, and they felt that their charter did not extend beyond the technology. In most instances designers are not trained to deal with organizational change.

Bjorn-Anderson and Hedberg argue for a broader scope and charter for a design team. They offer suggestions:

1. Train a designer to appreciate the organizational aspects of systems analysis and design.
2. Create more diversity in the composition of a design team.
3. Consider using dialectic problem solving techniques to generate more alternatives.

4. Emphasize performance measures which reflect the technology and human design objectives along with the economic.
5. Use rewards to encourage the design team to consider broad aspects of the systems proposed.

The authors point out that these steps are not enough and that users also have to be prepared to participate in systems analysis and design. Users need education about the technology. Such education will help to provide users with the needed self-confidence to participate in design and hopefully the motivation to insist on a role in this process.

Hoyer (1980) has also pointed out several constraints to greater end-user participation in design. One of the most severe is the ideology of the organization. It is very possible that any form of participation will not succeed if the organization itself is against it. One necessary task in bringing about more involvement will be to convince management that it is desirable.

STUDIES OF THE KOLB–FROHMAN MODEL

I shall further discuss the Kolb–Frohman process model itself in the next chapter. The model stresses the relationship between the consultant and the client in a change effort. The model consists of stages each of which features a different activity and relationship between client and consultant.

During scouting, the client and consultant are exploring a potential relationship. From scouting, the consultant seeks to find a formal entry point in the organization. During diagnosis, the problems in the organization are identified. The planning stage features the development of an approach to solving the problems identified earlier. The action stage applies the plans to the problems. During evaluation the consultant and client estimate the success of their efforts while termination marks the end of the relationship between consultant and client.

The United Farm Workers

Lucas and Plimpton (1972).   The authors present a case study on the design of a computer-based system by the United Farm Workers Organizing Committee. Because of the voluntary nature of this organization and its status as a quasi-civil rights, quasi-labor movement, the authors were concerned over their impact and the impact of any potential system on the union. This concern motivated careful attention to the relationship with the union as well as the task.

Prior to undertaking any steps associated with the task, the researchers assessed attitudes using a highly structured interview. The results showed a consensus in the union on the two departments most in need of improved information processing precedures. Unfortunately, these two departments were the least prepared attitudinally for a computer-based information system. The researchers took extreme care in establishing relationships with these two offices.

The preliminary survey also showed that the union leadership had by far the most favorable attitudes and were most optimistic about the potential of a computer-based system. Given this knowledge the researchers were able to explain the potential problems resulting from a computer-based system rather than to extoll the virtues of computer systems. Without this information the consultants could have attempted to sell a computer system and thus increase expectations that were already probably too favorable.

As part of the strategy the authors first conducted a feasibility study to determine if a computer system would be desirable for the union. Upon conclusion of that study the union and the researchers determined that a system was desirable. However, in keeping with the strategy of minimum change and impact, the designers worked with the union to develop a simple system and to encourage heavy user influence.

After a rough sketch of the system was completed, a review meeting was held with all union administrative staff members at a union retreat. The head of the union introduced the researchers and emphasized that no one would lose his or her job as a result of the development of a computer-based system. The authors indicated that the meeting would be a success only if half the system were changed. The presentation avoided the use of elaborate flip charts; instead the researchers worked from rough notes and used a blackboard and easel. The authors began with an explanation of possible output reports and worked backward to the processing logic files and finally the input for the system. The union responded very positively and suggested many changes to the rough system.

The authors had developed a very basic transactions processing system. Two weeks after the review meeting, the leaders of the union suggested reports of a managerial nature they wished to include to augment the basic system. The union was able to obtain volunteer programmers who worked full time to develop the system. Computer time was also donated by a service bureau that specialized in union pension fund processing. The system was successfully installed with minimum further interaction between the Union staff and the authors.

The stages in the Kolb–Frohman model were helpful in explaining the consultants' approach to this task after the completion of the project. First, a technically simple system was designed that would create the minimum change and have the greatest probability of working. The consultants measured attitudes toward a potential computer system in advance and considered the expectations of leaders and resistance in two key departments in planning their approach to the system. The authors also administered a second questionnaire to assess their impact prior to beginning programming of the system.

The consultants did not try to incorporate management reports; rather users suggested their own which fit their decision style and personal and situational factors. Personal and situational factors also influenced the design because the consultants tried to consider the uniqueness of the union, volunteers, and the nature of the staff in designing a simple, efficient system.

While the Kolb–Frohman was not used to guide the project, it proved very valuable in explaining the relationship between designers and users. The designers here focused on developing user ownership of the system.

A Multi-Project Study

Ginzberg (1979).   Ginzberg collected data from management scientists and users on 29 information system in 11 organizations. The projects could be classified on a continuum according to their complexity. Low complexity systems handled routine accounting jobs, while an example of a high complexity application would be a model-based management system.

The major hypothesis of the study was that success in implementation would be associated with the quality of the implementation process. Ginzberg developed a questionnaire to test the Kolb–Frohman model of implementation. The items on the questionnaire measured activities at each stage in the design process. The dependent variable in the study was overall satisfaction with the project.

Ginzberg found disagreement between designers and users on the rating of successful projects. Users reported eight cases where they were dissatisfied while designers indicated only four cases in which they felt users were dissatisfied. The intersection of the two, however, was only two cases. For user/designer pairs (in 27 of the cases), where the users were dissatisfied, the user and the designer disagreed on their responses on the process of implementation. This finding suggests a lack of communications or understanding between users and designers.

Users rated successful projects more highly on each of the Kolb–Frohman's stages than unsuccessful projects. By far the greatest differences occurred at the termination stage. In other words more successful projects were rated significantly better in the termination stage than unsuccessful projects. There was little evidence from the study that there were any differences across stages for projects of different complexity.

Summary

The United Farmworkers and Ginzberg studies suggest the importance of the relationship between the designers and users. The termination of this relationship should result in the user having psychological ownership of the system. At the same time the implementor needs to be concerned with the tasks of systems analysis and design.

OTHER PROCESS STUDIES

Field Centered Implementation

Ginsberg and Ramsey (1975).   The study suggests a field-centered approach to implementation that stresses mutual learning. The authors argue that designer centered approaches make unrealistic assumptions about each party, the user and the designer. Their approach was applied to the design of a loan pricing model for a West Coast bank. The authors began with a simple model and built on it as users made requests. The approach was evolutionary and stressed joint learning by designers and users.

A Motivational Model*

Vertinsky, Barth, and Mitchell (1975).   The authors present an implementation model for operations research and management science studies based on an expectancy-instrumentality-

---

* This study is hard to classify; the motivational model approaches a factor study, but most of the evidence presented deals with implementation as a social change process and the costs and benefits of change.

valence theory of motivation. The basic view of this model is of implementation as a social change process. The model consists of a number of parts: expectancy of type I is a manager's expectations that the use of an OR/MS model will lead to desired outcomes, for example, improved performance or decision making. This expectancy is influenced by the manager's self-esteem and previous experience.

Expectancy of type II refers to the manager's belief that tasks performed will lead to the desired outcomes or payoffs. This expectancy is influenced by individual differences and feedback on the perceived intensity of the connection between performance and payoff.

Valence refers to the manager's preference for different kinds of payoff contingent on performance. The theory predicts that expectancy and valence combine in a function of some type to determine motivation. The functional relationship linking these variables changes according to the circumstances of the OR study. Several other variables are included in this rather complex model. Evidence from an interview and questionnaire study of firms in western Canada led to the development of the model. Respondents in the study indicated that potential payoff was an important aspect of motivation. Another benefit expressed is immediate payoff from visibly improved performance. Some managers also received intrinsic rewards from experimentation with new techniques.

The most important costs were territorial threats, differences in approaches between OR/MS and traditional management, and power from information. A trusting relationship between the OR/MS groups and users led to the socialization of both groups creating changes in points of view. The authors concluded that:

1. Operations research solutions leading to significant social change tend to mobilize counter forces opposing the change.
2. Forced use of a system is clearly counter-productive.
3. The level of motivation to use OR/MS techniques influences the strategy to be followed in reducing dif-

ferences between the user's style and operations research techniques.

4. Good relationships between OR/MS practitioners and users depend on the motivation to use these techniques and interpersonal competence of the OR/MS staff.

5. Quantitatively-oriented users have a greater likelihood of accepting OR projects.

This motivational treatment of implementation as a social change process provides insights on the problems of the user. Do the costs to the user outweigh the benefits of a system? Vertinsky et al. also consider the factor of decision style in implementation. However, their model is complex and difficult to apply.

Implementation as a Change Process

Narasimhan and Schroeder (1979). The authors propose a model of implementation as a change process. These authors conducted an empirical study following the guidelines of a model of implementation. Their research framework suggests that management science intervention and organizational factors affect a decision system, which consists of information, the decision maker, the decision process and an outcome. Management science intervention impacts information, the decision maker and the decision process.

The authors collected empirical data for eight cases in business organizations. The cases were selected to reflect differences in factors expected to influence implementation. The researchers collected data from these organizations through questionnaires and some semistructured interviews with OR/MS practitioners and managers. Two case studies are described in detail in their paper.

In all eight cases management science intervention created more formal methods, a systems point of view, an explicit treatment of uncertainty and more comprehensive analysis of alternatives than prior approaches to decision making. The major impact of the project was in the evaluation of the choice phase of decision making. Where the OR staff and managers worked closely together, decision makers reported increased understanding of the problem, improved ability to use a structured approach and a greater degree of common information about problems. Other changes included more favorable perceptions of management science, higher degrees of cooperation, consensus on the important aspects of the decision and greater ability to communicate about the decision.

Questionnaires from 24 of the subjects were analyzed using factor analysis, which produced eight factors including work relationships, acceptance of recommendations, top management support and involvement, effort and time of the scientist, resources, goal definition, peer group influence, and technical validity of approach. A correlation analysis showed working relationships and technical validity were the most important factors affecting changes in the decision process.

The authors propose a more elaborate model of the change process of implementation as a result of their study. Management science intervention is the primary change agent while organizational factors exert a significant indirect influence on changes. Changes in the perspectives of decision makers appeared to precede changes in the decision process. Change is hierarchical occurring in stages each of which influences succeeding stages.

This study is important because it applies data analysis to a process model. There are multiple case studies which increase our confidence in the results. However, even with this design, the sample size is small for generalizing to other situations.

A Learning Model

Boland (1976). Boland conducted a study concerned with the interaction between designers and users during the definition of a problem (see also Boland 1978). The author defined two methods for interviews. In the interrogation method a traditional approach was used for requirements analysis; the designer was clearly in charge. In the interactive approach the designer and user both learned from the interview by reviewing information about each other. There is an opportunity to develop a working relationship and understanding of the other party while making progress on the task. The researchers analyzed these interviews to assess the amount of mutual understanding, amount of learning and quality of problem definition.

The study was a laboratory experiment employing a group of users (nurses) and professional system analysts from industry in a two person problem definition task involving the planning of an information system for a newly constructed hospital. Half of the team used the structured techniques of interrogation with the analyst as a leader, while the other half used the ill-structured technique of team dialog and shared leadership. Questionnaires and an expert panel were used to measure attitudes, the quality of the solutions proposed, and degree of mutual understanding and learning from the exercises.

There were no significant differences in the number of problems identified by the interogative or interactive analysts or by the groups as a whole. Nurses in the interactive group identified more problems than those in the interrogative group. The interactive teams had significantly higher idea quality scores than integrative groups.

The Boland study suggests one approach to client relationships and actions during requirements analysis. It suggests that we can learn about process through carefully designed laboratory experiments. The results also point out the importance of the relationship between designers and users and how this relationship can affect the task.

Implementation in Large Organizations

Manley (1976).   Manley found that the implementation process suitable for small organizations encounters difficulties in very large organizations like the Department of Defense. The author feels that attitude surveys are impractical and instead suggests a different type of implementation strategy called the large organization model building paradigm (LOMB). The approach is designed for organizations with tremendously large client populations which are rather ill-defined.

LOMB is constructed around an attitude object or "straw man." In Air Force terminology a "straw man" is an original document describing a change in policy, management practice, organizational alignment, contractual proceedings, engineering procedures, or any method of doing business. The "straw man" document is not final; recipients should review the document carefully.

The first iteration of the "straw man" usually reaches only a small group of interested professionals while the second round generally reaches a wider audience. Feedback is used to modify the document at each stage. If the results are positive the "straw man" is sent to the top and bottom levels in the organization. (Manley recommends that the model builder be located near the center of the organization.)

After informal agreement on the "straw man" by the entire organization the first formal proposal is drafted, which naturally generates organizational resistance. The "straw man" seeks to elicit a response from those interested in maintaining the status quo. Ad hoc working groups are appointed consisting of those in favor and opposed to a proposal. These groups form then develop a formal change plan.

Manley provides an example of this approach for developing a new and innovative Air Force regulation to extend established regulations covering general purpose computer system development into the weapon systems area.

The LOMB approach to implementation is very interesting and could be applied in other large organizations. However, many of the specifics in the example appear unique to the Department of Defense.

CONCLUSION

Our first conclusion from these process studies is that there is little published research of this type. The problem here is that very little incentive exists to publish process studies in the form of cases and there are few outlets for them. Cases are generally less rigorous in research methodology than factor studies because of small sample sizes and the lack of control and generalizability; they are difficult to publish in established journals. Practitioners in industry who are actively implementing system often do not have the time or motivation to publish their results. Undoubtedly there are many successful and unsuccessful implementation cases which remain unpublished from which we could gain many insights.

Empirical studies of the change process such as the one by Ginzberg are difficult to define and conduct. We shall probably see more of these in the future because of their importance in understanding the process of implementation.

The issues raised by the studies in this chapter are concerned with how systems are developed and their impact on organizations, work groups and individuals as illustrated by Mann and Williams. The Ginzberg and Lucas and Plimpton studies suggest that some shared control of the development process helps arrive at a termination stage where the system is owned by the user. Motivating managers to accept a system is a theme in Vertinski et al., while Boland suggests that the analyst and user learn from each other. Mumford advocates design through heavy user participation to maximize user satisfaction.

These studies show the need to consider the process of design and the relationship between the designer and user in addition to the design task itself. They point out that the user/designer relationship does impact the design task and is an important determinant of implementation success.

CHAPTER FIVE
A CONCEPTUAL FRAMEWORK

THE PURPOSE OF this chapter is to present a conceptual framework to organize the preceding discussion of implementation research and to guide actual implementation efforts in practice. The framework attempts to synthesize the factor and process approaches to implementation. Factor studies help us learn what variables are important in implementation while process studies explain how different variables influence implementation and suggest strategies to follow. The previous chapters have pointed out the importance of both types of research. These two paradigms are not opposed to each other; each has something to contribute to understanding and planning implementation.

Our goal is twofold; first to develop a framework that is consistent with the major research results reported earlier. Second it is important to present a scheme to help the designer plan for implementation. Our approach is to combine the most important factors with a process model and then to show how factors need to be considered at each stage in implementation.

FACTORS TO CONSIDER

Chapter 3 described a number of studies of factors related to implementation success. We saw how hundreds of variables

have been examined to find factors related to successful implementation. Clearly, this is far too large a number of factors
to consider in any implementation effort. However, these individual, operationalized variables can be grouped together into
generic classes of variables.*

Consider, for example, variables like a potential user's age,
educational status, length of time with the company, etc. There
are a number of ways to characterize an individual's personal
history and experience in an organization. To generalize from
these variables we can classify them as belonging to a class
labeled personal and situational factors. This characterization
of variables and their relationship to implementation success
calls the attention of the implementor to the importance of considerations like situational and personal variables. The implementor then determines which operationalized variables and
factors in this class are important for his or her specific system.
The remainder of this section discusses five important classes
of variables in implementation.

TECHNICAL CHARACTERISTICS OF SYSTEMS

Many of the factors related to implementation success are organizational and behavioral in nature. However, we have seen
the importance of variables related to the technical characteristics and qualities of a computer-based information system in
determining success. Technical considerations can be divided
into two classes: those absolutely mandatory for success and
those which greatly enhance the appeal and usefulness of a
system, though the line between these classes is not distinct.
Variables in the first category are necessary for success, but
not sufficient. They include characteristics like the accuracy of
input and output, reliability of an online system, the completion
of processing on schedule for a batch system, etc.

---

* A factor may consist of a single variable or a combination of variables. In this chapter,
I form groupings of factors to define broader classes like "attitudes". I shall continue
the common usage of "variable" and "factor" as synonymous.

The second type of technical variable is related to characteristics which are responsible for creating user satisfaction with a system and which encourage voluntary use of the system. Such variables include the design of the interface between the user and the system, for example, how difficult is it to provide input or to interpret output? What kind of terminals are used and what is the user's interaction with them? Are batch output reports clear, can they be understood easily?

There is overlap between the two subclasses of technical quality variables. The first set can be thought of as the base level of technological quality necessary for a system to work and be useable. Beyond that point technical quality enhances satisfaction with the system and stimulates voluntary use. Extra quality is not required but it may encourage use and satisfaction with the system.

Client Actions

Two variables in the client action class were extremely important in the research studies: management support and user involvement and influence. Management serves a leadership role in the organization and management support and attention are extremely important in implementation. Management also controls resources which are necessary to develop successful computer-based information systems.

Other individuals in the organization look to managers for cues; what behavior are managers trying to encourage? What behavior will be rewarded? If top management lacks knowledge of systems and is uninterested in them, then others will follow their model and implementation will be difficult or impossible.

Management also aids system development by making adequate resources available. These resources may be added personnel to free user time for design, an adequate systems staff and equipment, etc. Also the manager's own commitment of time to systems development is significant.

User involvement and influence is important in the implementation of information systems for several reasons. Much of the popular literature in the information systems field calls for involvement, but does not suggest how to achieve it. Involvement must mean influence or it is meaningless. The term "influence" implies that the user has an effect on the system.

Involvement results in systems of better quality because the user understands his or her job and information processing problems. It is too much to expect the analyst to be an expert in the development of a computer system, decision making in general, and the specific aspects of each decision maker's information processing tasks in the organization.

Involvement and influence can create more favorable attitudes. Individuals who have participated in decisions feel they own a part of the solution and are more favorable toward it. Users are better trained and more knowledgeable about systems when they have participated in their design; knowledge also makes conversion to and installation of a new system easier.

Participation is treated here as a factor, but it also is a link to the process of design. We shall discuss it further in the next section.

Attitudes Toward Systems

We are interested in attitudes toward information systems because attitudes usually have an action component. We expect an individual with a certain attitude is likely to take action in certain situations. There is, however, much debate over the nature of the relationship between attitudes and behavior. Most researchers agree that general attitudes are not a predictor of specific behavior. In the context of information systems, knowing a user's general attitude toward automation probably is not a good predictor of how the user will respond to a new on-line system.

However, the research in chapter 3 suggested that an attitude toward a specific stimulus like the input and output quality of a computer system is a good predictor of the use of a voluntary system or satisfaction with a mandatory system. To distinguish between general attitudes and those toward a specific object seems reasonable. The experience one has with the typical computer-based system is quite personal and less subject to social approval and group influence than, say, an attitude toward a politician or a political party. The attitude toward a system and behavior toward it is not as likely to be influenced by colleagues as much as a general attitude.

Decision Style

Decision style is the characteristic way we have of approaching a decision problem; for example, some individuals like quantitative information while others prefer more prose. Research on variables in this class show that they are important in implementation, however, identifying specific variables has proven to be difficult.

One finds variations among different individuals approaches to problems based on this decision style. The sensing-thinking individual is very analytical and is interested in a detailed picture while an intuitive-feeling problem solver is not concerned with details. We expect these different characteristic ways of approaching a problem to influence the use of computer-based information systems, for example, a factual report with many numbers would probably appeal to a sensing-thinking individual.

Clearly variables like cognitive style and complexity are important. There is also an ethical question which must be considered in addressing decision style; to what extent should the systems designer take cognitive style into account and design for it and to what extent should the designer (or does the designer have the right) to attempt to change the user's cognitive style through an information system? We shall discuss this question further later in the chapter.

Personal and Situational Variables

We saw earlier that variables like age, education, length of time in the company, etc. seemed to be important based on implementation research. Consider a branch manager for a bank in which the information systems department has just developed a new report describing the demographic characteristics of the neighborhood in which the branch is located. How would this report be used by a new branch manager, who recently graduated with an MBA and a twenty year veteran of the bank who has been at the same branch for fifteen years? The new MBA would probably be very happy to receive the report. The veteran manager, however, undoubtedly knows everyone in the neighborhood and most likely would not find the report very helpful.

These and similar situational and personal variables can greatly influence the success of implementation for a given individual or even a class of individuals. The difficulty comes in characterizing each situation since factors are often unique for a specific computer-based system.

RELATIONSHIP AMONG FACTORS

We anticipate that the factors discussed are related to each other and to successful implementation. See figure 5.1 for one possible model of this relationship. Technical characteristics are expected to influence successful implementation as defined by measures of systems use and user satisfaction with the system. A system must be of sufficient technical quality that it can be used as discussed earlier. Technical characteristics are also expected to influence user attitudes since technical aspects of the system affect users directly when working with it.

Client action should influence implementation directly and through its impact on user attitudes. For example, management support encourages the user to work on the development of a system. Decision style influences attitudes and has a strong

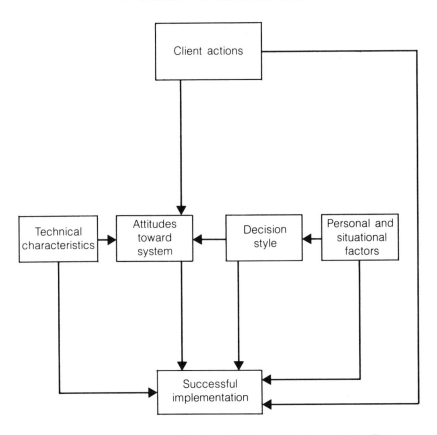

Figure 5.1   Hypothesized Relationship Among Implementation Factors

influence on use and satisfaction with the system. There are other possible relationships among these factors, but the ones in figure 5.1 seem to represent both the most important and the simplest links among the variables.

IMPLEMENTOR INFLUENCE

Figure 5.2 places the classes of factors we have discussed above on a continuum showing the amount of influence the implementor has over each.

Figure 5.2 Implementor Influence Over Various Implementation Factors

Technology

The greatest influence of the implementor is over the technological characteristics of a system. The analyst is a technical expert and can control the technology employed. The analyst is constrained by budgets and often by available computer equipment: however, these constraints are not too severe given the great flexibility and declining cost of modern technology.

Client Actions

The analyst can influence general attitudes toward and perceptions of an information system including at least two important variables in this class: management support and user involvement. The analyst can assess the possible lack of management support in advance and take steps to gain support. The implementor can also try to influence management to take the action necessary to facilitate implementation.

The implementor usually has a say in the extent of user involvement and influence on a system. The major constraints on involvement are:

1. The willingness of the analyst to involve users

2. User time constraints

3. Users' feelings of their own confidence and ability to help in the design process

4. Management encouragement of user influence, for example, provision for additional resources to reduce some of the user's existing commitments

5. Incentives for the user to participate (what will the individual gain and what will it cost?)

Attitudes Toward the System

Attitudes are difficult to influence directly: we expect that a high quality technical system will tend to improve user attitudes since attitudes are developed through experience, peer group influence, etc. By working with management support, taking user desires into account in developing a system, and designing a system with high technical quality, the implementor expects to influence the formation of favorable user attitudes as shown in figure 5-1. However, to the extent that attitudes exist and are negative due to past unpleasant experience with computer-based systems, the implementor of a new system will have difficulty altering these attitudes.

Decision Style

In the short run it is very difficult to influence the decision style of decision makers, though, in the long run the use of a system may influence decision style. Some systems may have the exclusive goal of modifying the decision style of users. We must ask whether or not this is desirable or even possible. By trying to alter decision style, we are manipulating users and even changing personality characteristics of which we have little knowledge. (Decision style will be discussed further later in the chapter.)

Personal and Situational Factors

The implementor of an information system has very little control or influence over personal or situational variables especially in the short run: design instead must be contingent on these factors. The implementor might suggest that certain divisions not receive output for a system or users might be asked to design their own. In other words, we must accept most personal and situational factors and take them into account in the design process.

Conclusion

The implementor has control and influence over relatively few of the factors discussed so far. On the left side of figure 5.2, the implementor has the greatest influence and on the right side of the continuum, the best we can do is plan for implementation contingent on these factors. Of course, awareness of the existence of the uncontrollable factors should help; many designers have failed to recognize the presence and importance of these factors.

One element of great significance is missing from the discussion so far. This element is very much subject to the influence of the implementor; it is the process of design which refers to the relationship between the implementor and user or client. The process includes the planning of the change effort represented by implementation. By carefully considering the factors described above at each stage in the development process, one can increase the chances for the successful implementation of a computer-based information system.

ONE PROCESS MODEL

There are many different approaches to the general process of bringing about organizational change and to the implementation of new technology (see Schein 1969). We would like to adopt a model which includes consideration of the issues raised in our discussion of process research, namely the impact of a system on the organization's structure, work groups and individuals, control over the design process, successful termination of the relationship between the designer and user, motivation to use a new system and mutual learning by the user and designer.

To accomplish these objectives, we shall adopt and modify a model of organizational change which we saw in chapter 4; it has been applied at least once in an implementation case study (Lucas and Plimpton 1972). This model was first proposed

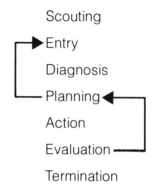

Scouting

Entry

Diagnosis

Planning

Action

Evaluation

Termination

Figure 5.3   A Process Model

by Kolb and Frohman (1970) (see figure 5.3). Of course, other models could be used, but the Kolb–Frohman model highlights important considerations in the process of implementation and it has been employed in implementation research.

A change agent is an individual or group that tries to introduce change into the organization smoothly. Because of the changes created by systems, designers function as change agents whether they realize it or not. The Kolb–Frohman model features a change agent or consultant and a client. For most information systems, the systems analyst functions much like a consultant because of his or her attachment to the highly specialized information services department. For some projects we should subdivide the "client" into two parts: management and the user. Again, in the information systems environment often these individuals are the same or both managers and users in affected areas are aware of systems development. However, we should also be sensitive to the situation in which the manager authorizes a system for users who did not request it.

The model focuses on two key concepts: the relationship between the implementor and users and the nature of the implementation task itself. Too many times computer professionals have only been concerned with a task and have ignored this relationship.

Scouting

The stages in the Kolb–Frohman model are not distinct; some stages may be entered several times as the feedback loops imply. The first stage, scouting, is characterized by the lack of commitment on either the part of implementor or the user. Each party tries to assess the motives of the other. A number of factors influence scouting, including the resources available, constraints, the motivation of the other party, etc. The computer professional may not want to develop a system if there are too many constraints and too few resources.

Entry

The initial relationship between the implementor and users should result in the determination of a formal entry point in the organization. Who is the primary user of a system? Now the user and implementor negotiate a contract. The contract may not be a formal document containing costs and guarantees; rather there is a psychological contract showing expectations and goals for a system. Agreement is needed on goals for a project; we should attempt to develop a broad definition of the project, the resources available, the method of approaching the design, the benefits from the final product and the nature of the relationship between the implementor and user.

   The initial relationship between the implementor and the client is probably based on the expert power of the computer professional. Hopefully expert-based power will change to trust and collaborative problem solving during the process of design.

Diagnosis

During diagnosis, the goals of the user are to define the system in more detail. A feasibility study for an information system would be a typical result from this stage. The implementor also is thinking about the client relationship and assessing the readiness of the client to develop a system. What is the nature of the information processing problem? What subunits in the organization are involved? Who are the users? One task here is to delineate the resources of the user and implementor to undertake the project.

Planning

The planning stage includes both technical details of the system and the relationship between the user and implementor. What is to be accomplished by what dates? How is the relationship to proceed? What will be the composition of the design team for a system? How do we plan for the impact of the system on potential users and on what factors is successful implementation contingent?

Action

The project is developed during the action stage; here we must be particularly concerned with the ultimate acceptance of the system. Users may be motivated to cooperate in developing a system from expectations that use will lead to a desired outcome according to Vroom's (1964) model of motivation. The model states that the force to act, i.e., motivation, is a multiplicative function of valence and instrumentality. Valence is the desire for a particular outcome, such as high pay. Instrumentality is the expectation that some behavior like high production will lead to the desired outcome.

 The model predicts that if either valence or instrumentality is 0, there will be no motivation. If a worker does not desire more pay then there will be no motivation to work harder, all other factors being equal. Similarly if the perceived probability that productivity leads to high pay is 0, there will be no motivation to produce more.

Before applying the Vroom model to implementation we need to discuss Lewin's theory of change. Lewin conceptualized change as a movement in an equilibrium; see figure 5.4. An equilibrium is maintained by forces operating in two directions; one to encourage change and the other to inhibit it. Change can be effected by reducing the inhibiting forces, increasing the forces encouraging change or some combination of these two approaches. Zand and Sorensen (1975) provide evidence on the applicability of the Lewin theory to implementation, as discussed in chapter 2.

There are three phases to the planned change activity of the action stage:

1. Unfreezing increases the receptiveness of the user to change; forces maintaining equilibrium are modified to prepare for change. Forces impeding change are

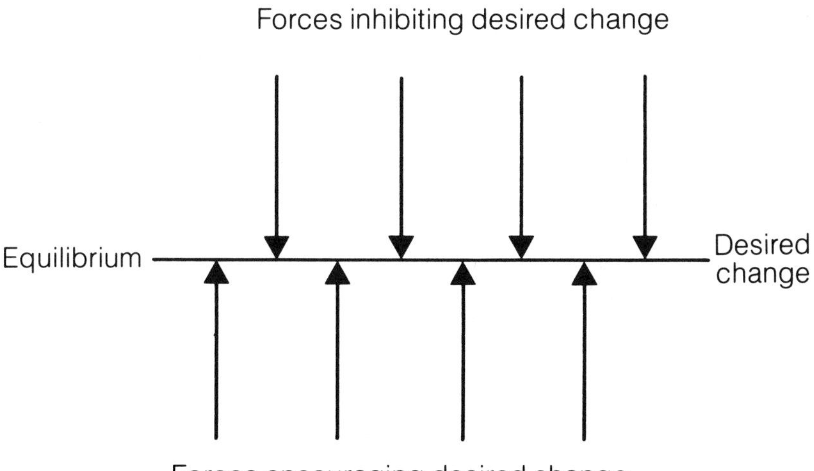

Figure 5.4 The Lewin Force Field

reduced and/or forces encouraging change are strengthened. To some extent we have already accomplished this process if users have requested a system.

2. Moving is the actual change itself; changes in forces for the change and against it shift the equilibrium point to a new, desired level.

3. Refreezing is reinforcing a change so the new equilibrium is maintained.

How can we apply the Vroom and the Lewin models to implementation? We want to motivate users to help design and work with a system. We need to encourage the formation of user expectations that cooperation and participation and use will lead to desired outcomes. These perceived outcomes of the system then become the forces driving or initiating change.

The Vroom model is constructed in terms of positive or 0 valence, that is, an outcome is or is not desired. In the Lewin model there are inhibiting forces as well which we can think of as being highly undesirable outcomes or negative valences. The favorable outcomes are benefits of the system and negative outcomes represent costs. The positive forces for any system depend on the nature of the system itself. They may include better information, faster response, cost reduction, etc.

Costs or inhibiting forces also depend on the system, but for any implementation effort we predict that certain costs will usually be perceived by the user including:

Fear of change in the structure of the organization, work groups and personal behavior

Uncertainties about one's own ability to perform with a new system

Fears of unknown power shifts

Uncertainties about how to use the new system

In general the changes which represent expected undesirable outcomes from a system create a great deal of uncertainty for users. In fact for some outcomes the user is probably unsure whether the outcome is favorable or unfavorable; expectations are unstable.

Figure 5.5 depicts the situation we have just described. Our objectives of bringing about greater user participation, cooperation and system use can be accomplished by increasing the user's expectations that favorable outcomes will result from the system and decreasing expectations that outcomes will be unfavorable. Users should perceive that participation, cooperation and use will lead to the desired benefits from the system. That is, we are trying to increase the positive valence of system benefits and reduce the negative valence of system costs. We are also trying to show that participation, cooperation and system use are instrumental to accomplishing the highly desirable benefits of the system. If successful the motivation for change should be high.

The implementor could demonstrate the fact that a proposed system would reduce costs, produce better information and/or lead to greater efficiencies. The more credible the demonstration, the higher the valence of the outcomes. Then the implementor could try to show that only through participation in design, cooperation and the eventual use of a system will these benefits be realized. Management support and involvement in design will also increase user perceptions of system benefits.

The implementor should also deal with the costs of the system and try to lessen their negative valence. One possibility would be to make desired behavior instrumental to reducing the costs of the system. For example, the implementor could stress that participation and cooperation in the design of the system will help the user reduce uncertainties, influence power shifts and gain confidence in the use of the system.

Figure 5.5 also demonstrates how the benefits of a system sometimes accrue to those who do not bear its costs and vice versa. The benefits of greater efficiency and reduced costs probably are realized by the organization installing the system, rather than an individual user. However the costs of using the

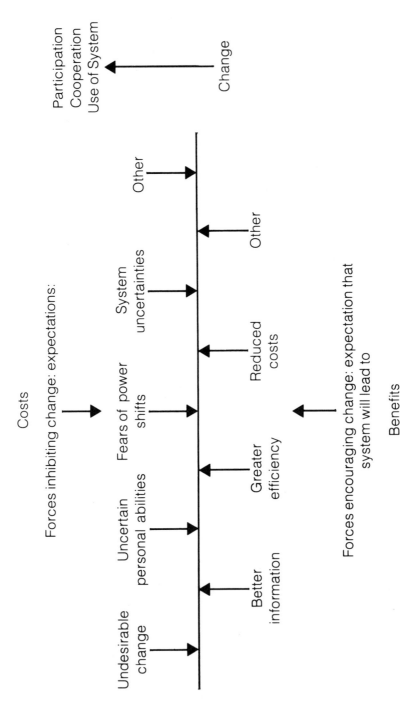

Figure 5.5 Expectancy and Change Theories Applied to Implementation

system in terms of uncertainty, power shifts and coping with change are borne by the individuals who work regularly with it. In other instances, users who work with a badly designed interface inputting data may receive none of the benefits of rapid information retrieval; the positive results of the system are enjoyed by a different group of users who do not have to confront the poor input interface.

Evaluation

In the evaluation stage of the Kolb–Frohman model the results of the change are examined honestly. Here we should look at the task and relationship between implementor and the user. The results of evaluation suggest changes to existing projects and should certainly contribute to planning future systems.

Termination

The last stage in implementation and possibly the most important is termination. The idea here is to end successfully what has been a temporary relationship between the implementor and the user. We feel that the most successful termination for an information systems development project occurs when the user has developed psychological ownership of the system. Termination, rather than being considered only as the final stage, must be continuously considered from the initiation and scouting phases through the very end of the development process.

This model of the consultant client relationship is well suited to describing the steps which occur in the implementation of a computer-based information system. More importantly it points out several key considerations that emerged from our discussions of process research and the implementation of systems. First, the model does focus on the process and the relationship between the designer and user. At each stage in the model, the task is also considered, though the primary focus is on the relationship aspects of implementation.

The model recognizes that implementation is a change activity, and that we must consider the motivation of a user to change. It explicitly deals with the question of control. The designer and the user are jointly responsible for the development of the system. During scouting and entry the value systems of each party are explored. By placing great emphasis on termination, the Kolb–Frohman model suggests that we must consider the ownership of a system. If the designer is to successfully terminate a relationship with the user, then formal ownership of a system must be in the users' hands.

A CONCEPTUAL FRAMEWORK

The major classes of factors developed earlier in this chapter are important, but they seem to ignore significant parts of the process of design and are too static. On the other hand, the Kolb–Frohman model is quite general and focuses on the relationship between the designer and the user. It is possible to lose sight of the taks if only the Kolb–Frohman model is followed. In this section we seek to synthesize these two approaches into one, common framework. Our objective is to develop a conceptual model which simultaneously allows us to focus on the process of design and the design task.

Table 5.1 arrays the factors discussed earlier against the stages of the Kolb–Frohman model. We are combining the factors in the model of figure 5.1 with the process model in figure 5.3. Our objective is to demonstrate how the various factors influence each stage in the implementation process and how they should be taken into account in an actual implementation effort involving the analysis and design of a new computer-based information system.

Scouting

During this stage the analyst and user are exploring the potential relationship and examining resources. From a technical

Table 5.1 An Implementation Framework

Stages	Technical Characteristics	Client Action	Factors		
			Attitudes Toward System	Decision Style	Personal, Situational Factors
Scouting Entry	Need Goals Boundaries	Observe Enlist support Involvement	Observe Observe	Observe Observe Assess Impact	Observe Delineate
Diagnosis	Feasibility	Formalize support Involvement Form design team	Assess formally	Assess formally Reflect in goals	Assess formally Reflect in goals
Planning (project-process)	Resources Schedule	Delineate resources needed for change Management action	Expected reactions	Incorporate alternatives, diff. styles Assess impact	Plan for different conditions
Action Unfreeze Change Refreeze	Delineate system Specify program Convert	Management action User teams Added resources Reward structure	Costs/benefits of change Group influence Group commitment	Include different styles in plans Different alternatives in system Tailored training Conversion	Design contingent Reflect in specs Tailored training and conversion
Evaluation	Modify	Through design plan Required mgt. action	Assess and reinforce	Contingent on styles Relative to goals	Contingent on factors Relative to goals
Termination	High levels of use	Diffusion to others Continued mgt. support	User commitment Ownership High satisfaction	Widespread user ownership	Widespread user ownership

Design activities to consider factors at each stage

standpoint the purpose is to assess the need for a system. The analyst should carefully observe attitudes of the potential system user and the level of management support. Also, what is the outlook for a widespread user involvement and influence on design? The analyst should look for differences in personal and situational factors for potential users. Decision style is hard to observe and the analyst should be prepared for and expect differences among users and the way they approach problems.

Entry

At this point the analyst and user are developing at least a psychological contract, if not one in legal terms. What does each party expect from the other? Technically we must be able to state the preliminary goals and boundaries for the system. The analyst should continue to observe the attitudes of potential users to determine if the system is organizationally feasible. Active management support should be enlisted here. The analyst should indicate what actions and resources are needed from management. Can the type of user involvement desired be arranged? The analyst should have a clear picture now of the situational factors which exist and an idea of different personal factors which might influence the design process. The goals of the system should be clear making it possible to estimate the impact of the system on the decision style of potential users and vice versa.

Diagnosis

Diagnosis involves an assessment of the technical feasibility of the proposed system and a reassessment of the goals of the system. At this point an attempt should be made to formally survey attitudes through interviews or questionnaires. From the standpoint of general attitudes and perceptions, it is necessary to formalize management support by defining concrete action steps for management. The bases and mechanism for user involvement and influence should also be established and a design team formed. The analyst and newly formed design team should formally assess personal and situational factors. If decision style appears important, it should also be explored at this time.

Planning

We must plan for two parts of the system: 1) the technical capability for the system; and 2) the process of how the system is to be designed. Technically, we are interested in the resources required and a schedule to complete the traditional steps in systems analysis and design, including analysis of the present system, developing the design specification, programming, testing and installation.

Process considerations are of interest to the design team; it should plan for the expected reactions of potential users. The support the team needs for management and special resources are also determined here. The design team plans a strategy for different personal and situational factors and for decision style. Based on research results, we recommend extensive user influence on design decisions. It may be desirable at this point to make an inventory for each potential user showing his or her situational factors, attitudes, decision style, etc., and how the system will impact these variables.

Action

The action stage includes unfreezing, changing, and refreezing. Technically this process is associated with development of the system, preparation of specifications, programming and conversion. From the process standpoint, the costs and benefits for individual users must be clear. A good technical design creates benefits or positive outcomes and we must see that users expect these benefits. Management support helps suggest that users will be rewarded for their cooperation.

Heavy user participation helps reduce inhibiting forces and expectations of undesirable outcomes. Through participation the user learns about the system reducing uncertainties about its final form and functions. Participation helps the user gain control over the system rather than lose power and influence in the organization. Participation in planning organizational, group and individual changes helps create understanding of the need for change and reduces uncertainty about whether outcomes will be favorable or unfavorable. Lucas (1974) even suggests that users should be in charge of the design process while the analyst becomes a catalyst and guide in the design process.

Some researchers in the field have suggested developing a detailed balance sheet for each individual predicting the costs and benefits from a change for that person. If the cost side of the ledger is too high and/or benefits are too low, the system may have to be modified to provide an incentive for use. Once in finalized form, the balance sheet can be used to make clear the benefits to the individual and indicate what changes are needed; it can serve as a valuable check list for training as well. Remember to prepare the balance sheet by individual since often the costs of a system are incurred by one group and the benefits are enjoyed by another!

During the action stage, the influence of the potential user group and the design team is used to develop a compatible system and to enlist commitment to it. Compatibility means that design takes into account different personal and situational factors and decision styles. The design team may also require specific management action and additional resources to complete the system and changes in the reward structure to encourage system use.

Evaluation

Evaluation of a computer-based information system after its installation is frequently lacking. Often projects are late and over budget and individuals are eager to begin something new. An evaluation should, however, be conducted. It may show that it is necessary to modify some of the technical aspects of the design. The design team should assess user attitudes toward the system after the trauma of conversion is over. They should work to reinforce positive attitudes by changing systems or procedures to meet complaints, criticism and suggestions wherever possible. The design team evaluates the success of management action and its own performance, a process which should suggest changes and possibly further management action. How were original goals modified? Did personal and situational factors or decision styles necessitate changes in plans?

Termination

The entire design effort has been aimed a successful termination, high levels of systems use and user satisfaction. The ownership of the system should be shared by all users. A system designed contingent upon personal and situational factors and decision style should encourage user satisfaction. A process of design which stresses these concerns is intended to produce user ownership of the system and commitment to it.

A Note on Decision Style

As the review of implementation factors pointed out, we have evidence that decision style is an important variable in implementation. However, the research results are not consistent and a priori predictions about decision style are difficult. At some point as the desired system becomes clarified during entry or diagnosis, it should be possible to predict the potential impact of the system on the decision style of the major users.

We suggest the following guidelines for attempting to change decision style.

1. If possible design a system which does not require

any changes in the decision style of users for success. In these instances take decision style into account and make design contingent on it.

2. Try to make organizational and behavioral changes prior to the development of the system. These changes are complex enough that they should not be linked to a new system. Users who are uncomfortable with change may perceive the system as the causal mechanism and thus develop antagonism toward it.

3. Make the desired changes and reasons for them open and obvious.

4. Try to show the users the benefits of change, be honest about personal costs.

5. Be sure that changes will be an improvement.

Figure 5.6 is a flowchart of the above recommendations in detail. Examples of possible systems include:

1. An order entry application requiring no change in decision style since there is little decision making involved in this transactions processing system.

2. A subsystem to output the results from a planning model. The model output is not designed to change the decision style of the user. However, different approaches to output need to be considered, for example, tabular reports, graphics, drawings, scenarios, etc.

3. A reorder point-reorder quantity approach to purchasing. A change in decision style is desired and the information system merely facilitates it. The system is not the reason for the change, rather management has decided change is needed. Consider a group of purchasing agents adopting a reorder point-reorder quantity approach to purchasing. A change program could be conducted by management prior to developing and

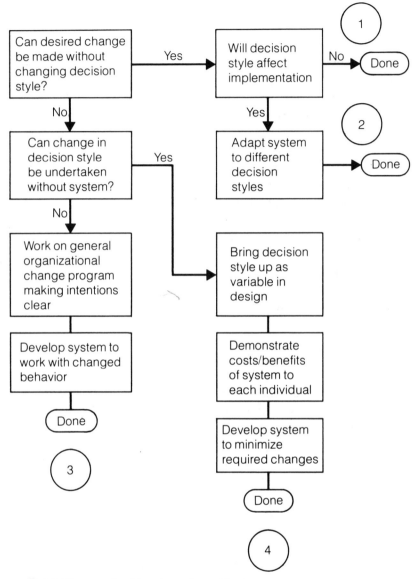

Example: 1. An order entry system.
2. Output routines for a planning model.
3. Purchasing agents using a new reorder point/quantity system.
4. Users learning to accept a quantitative planning model.

Figure 5.6   A Suggested Approach to Implementation Considering Decision Styles

installing a computer system to compute the desired quantities.

4. A quantitative planning model. Management wishes to change the decision style of many potential users who are not accustomed to data-based planning approaches. Cognitive style should be discussed and the benefits of change demonstrated to users. In this example advances by other firms employing such an approach could be stressed. A hypothetical planning system might also be maintained and compared to test the benefits of the new approach. The system should be designed finally to minimize changes in decision style; the important and necessary ones should be considered. We shall discuss an example later in which decision style was ignored and the desired goals of the system were not achieved.

SUMMARY

This chapter has presented a conceptual framework for implementation which combines both factors related to implementation and the process of developing an information system. The framework is designed to guide the implementation of computer-based information systems and discussions about implementation. The framework is consistent with the major theories of implementation and is supported by the factor and process studies as shown in table 5.2.

While not drawn directly from the theories and ideas of Zand and Sorensen, Schultz and Slevin, and Lucas, the conceptual model is consistent with their suggestions. Data from Lucas, the Northwestern studies, Swanson and the cognitive style researchers contribute the factors in the conceptual model. Many if not most of the factors identified in the factor research can be grouped into the categories suggested in table 5.1. Finally, the process model of our conceptual framework is

Table 5.2 Support For Framework of Table 2.1

Theories	Factor Studies	Process
Zand and Sorensen (1975)†	*Technical*	Mumford and Banks (1967)*
Schultz and Slevin (1977)†	Lucas (1973)	Mumford and Ward (1968)*
Lucas (1974)†	*Client Action*	Lucas and Plimpton (1972)†
	Northwestern Studies*	Ginzberg (1979)†
	Lucas (1978a and b)†	Boland (1976)*
	Attitudes	Mumford and Henshall (1979)*
	Lucas (1975a and b, 1976)*	
	Swanson (1974)†	
	Decision Style	
	Huysmans (1970)†	
	Doktor and Hamilton (1973)*	
	Mitroff, Nelson, and Mason (1974)†	
	Personal Situational	
	Lucas (1975a and b, 1976)*	

* Moderate support.
† Strong support.

highly consistent with the work of Mumford and is supported by the Lucas and Plimpton, and Ginzberg studies. Boland also provides evidence to support this approach.

The model in table 5.1 will help the reader organize the research discussed so far in this text. In the next chapter, two examples are discussed and analyzed with the framework to show that it can be of analytic value. Another objective of the model is to help those involved in actual implementation efforts. The model can guide implementation by focusing the attention of the analyst on crucial factors during the different stages of systems development. It stresses dual concerns with the design task and the relationship between users and the designers of a system.

CHAPTER SIX
TWO EXAMPLES

THIS CHAPTER presents an application of the conceptual framework of chapter 5 to two case studies of implementation: one partially successful and the other apparently very successful. The framework is first used to show what factors were considered by the designers at each stage and as a basis for comparing the two case studies. These two case are intended to illustrate the ideas in the monograph and the application of the results of the research reviewed in chapters 2 through 4.

A PORTFOLIO MANAGEMENT SYSTEM

Banks and other financial institutions in the United States manage large amounts of assets. Their portfolios generally consist of stocks, fixed income securities and cash or the equivalent. In 1976 the *New York Times* published a survey of the ten largest institutional investors in the United States which showed combined assets in excess of $240 billion.

A bank trust department is staffed with trust investment officers who manage one or more portfolios, usually for a fee based on the net asset value of the portfolio at a given point in time. There are a number of different types of investors who establish trusts, each having different goals, for example growth, income, return, etc. The evaluation of investment performance is very difficult given this variety of investment objectives.

Most banks have several lists of securities which are approved for investment. The bank's own research department or external research organizations furnish the information about individual securities in the form of company or industry reports. The bank accounting department produces reports of the status of each portfolio, showing the securities held by the account and their market value on at least a monthly basis. Security prices, the other information needed to manage portfolios, are available from a wide variety of sources such as newspapers or the stock exchange tapes.

A Prototype System

Gerrity (1971).   As a part of his Ph.D. dissertation, Gerrity developed an on-line, graphics-based time-sharing system to assist trust investment officers in making investment decisions. Gerrity's study showed that one third of the time of the trust investment officer was spent in customer contact, one third in the review and revision of portfolios, and the remainder in the study of securities and market-related information. The objective of his system was to improve the availability and usefulness of three sources of information described above for making investment decisions.

There are a number of normative theories of portfolio management, though many of these are popular only in academic circles and have not been applied in actual investment organizations. Gerrity found in his initial studies that investment decisions were security-centered, that is, the trust officers focused on individual securities across all portfolios. One natural reason for this focus is the nature of the information the officer receives in the form of research on individual securities.

Regardless of whether the investment industry subscribes

to the full normative theories of portfolio management, most individuals accept the concept that the overall portfolio structure is important in determining the expected risk and return of the portfolio and hence, is important to the client.

Gerrity summarized the problems with the bank's current information system for trust officers:

1. The priced out portfolio status reports were too often out-of-date and had to be updated by hand.

2. The data base was fragmented into two separate files: one of portfolio holdings and the other of stock performance history and forecasts.

3. There was no aggregate, overall measure of portfolio status and structure.

4. There was no formal means for comparing portfolio status with goals.

5. The reports in the systems suffered from overly rigid formats.

6. There was a tendency to search very locally for stock candidates for purchase or sale. The entire list of nearly 350 approved stocks was seldom considered explicitly.

7. There was a lack of any formal mechanism for considering alternative portfolios.

8. The existing information system had an extremely slow response when reporting the holdings of stocks across all portfolios.

Gerrity reported that after a relatively short period of use of the prototype system, investment managers moved from security-oriented to more portfolio-oriented approaches to investment decisions. He found that session lengths averaged about an hour with the prototype and that 13 reports were requested. There was wide usage of functions; the maximum for any function was 21% use.

Stabell (1975). In a later study of the Gerrity system, Stabell interviewed managers after the system had been operational and examined the output of a monitor built into the system to trace command usage. He reports that the system was not used as originally intended, rather its major function appeared to be as a reporting tool to provide better and more up-to-date status reports. The system did not appear to figure heavily in the decision making process as the following data show.

	GERRITY *Prototype*	*STABELL* *Follow-up*
Session length	60 minutes	5 minutes
Number of reports requested	13	3
Maximum use of function	21% for one function	80% for two functions

Stabell suggests the following reasons for the pattern of use he observed.

1. Low manager capacity for change; historically the managers had relied on a limited number of sources of information.

2. A lack of a definition of the changes desired by management; it was not clear to the investment officers that portfolio-oriented decision making actually is best. Training was also limited to the mechanics of the system.

3. Lack of investment manager faith in the research data contained in the system.

4. The purchaser of the system, senior management, differed from the intended user, the trust officer.

It appears that the system was not as successful as hoped. An assumption was made that provided with a technical tool allowing portfolio-oriented decisions, managers would naturally adopt the new approach. There were no real incentives for the user; the costs of potential performance failures outweighed the probable benefits.

A Mature System

The prototype system above was refined and sold as a proprietary software product to another major bank. Alter (1975) describes the experiences of this bank with the system. There are four departments in the trust division of the bank which are important in the use of the system, including investment research, trusts and estates, pension and capital management.

Fifteen analysts worked for the investment research department which serves a staff function for the other three departments. These individuals are responsible for maintaining a list of approved stocks which the portfolio managers may buy for their accounts. The research staff also provides detailed analysis of particular stocks and industries.

Each of the portfolio managers was in one of three departments and responsibilities varied widely among the departments. In the trust and estate department managers usually handle a large number of accounts averaging some 160 though each account is relatively small. The main responsibility in this department is to assure that the funds are invested in accordance with the current economic outlook, the needs of the trust, and the investment policy of the bank. For estate accounts the bank also has additional duties such as collecting, conserving and distributing the estate according to the terms of the will. Within different geographical regions a great deal of competition exists for new trust or estate account business. Existing accounts, however, show little movement due to the personal relationship that develops between the portfolio manager and the client.

The pension divisions tend to be highly competitive and performance-oriented. Portfolio managers in this department usually manage only 10 to 15 funds and their performance is examined very closely. Pension funds are the largest handled by the bank. The client is aware of the investment decisions and these individuals are quite willing to move accounts to other trust departments if dissatisfied with performance. Some of the largest pension funds even split their capital among four or five trust departments and replace the worst performer each year with a new bank.

The capital management division furnishes investment advisory portfolio management services for wealthy individuals who tend to be aggressive investors and are willing to accept comparatively high risk to attain high growth in return. Approximately 30 accounts on the average are managed by trust officers in this area.

The goals of the different types of accounts vary widely. The trust and estates area tends to have accounts which are relatively conservative in nature; their primary objective is usually the preservation of capital rather than total return. Sometimes the discretion of the portfolio manager is limited by special provisions and requirements such as tax considerations, client bequests or guidelines, etc.

Capital management accounts tend to be much more aggressive than those in trust and estates, though they are also subject to special requirements. The greatest discretion allowed the portfolio manager comes from the performance sensitive pension accounts which are not subject to taxes. Clearly, the goals and responsibilities of portfolio management are not homogeneous across accounts; actions which are appropriate for one account may be inappropriate for another.

Competitiveness has become an extremely important factor in the portfolio management environment. Part of this competitive pressure has developed from the emergence of mutual funds, investment management services and other groups in the capital management field. Many banks have tried to change their relatively conservative image by demonstrating that they can also be progressive. Although there were many reasons for this bank acquiring the portfolio management system, competitive aspects of the environment provided two important motivations since the bank felt that advantages might be gained both in terms of actual performance and image.

In late 1969 the bank officer who now functions as a co-ordinator for the portfolio management system read an article in a trade magazine which described a portfolio system being developed for another bank. The officer invited the company developing the system to present a demonstration at his bank. In the spring of 1970 the initial feasibility study began. The study consisted of three phases; the first describing all potential functions for such a system, the second describing the value of particular functions which seem the most appropriate and the third a justification of the proposed system in monetary terms. A bank-wide priorities committee concurred with a trust department recommendation that the system be developed and a contract was signed in early 1971.

The cost/benefit study justified the system based primarily on a need for proportionally fewer managers as the portfolio business grew. The system also was expected to provide benefits in developing new business, improving profits from existing business, and improving performance in general. Some of the individuals in the study were motivated by estimated tangible benefits, while others focused on intangibles. Regardless of the underlying motivation the general feeling was that the system would help portfolio managers in a number of ways. An important consideration was that the system would provide the mechanics to examine alternative decisions. The manager would be able to do things which were impossible before or which took too long a time to be feasible. The manager could also do things with the system that currently had to be undertaken by support personal. No one saw the system as the ultimate decision maker, rather it was viewed as a system to assist the portfolio manager in evaluating alternative courses of action so that he or she could make the right decision.

Several existing on-line portfolio systems marketed by time-sharing houses were also examined in the study. However they would require modification and many had bad response time and rather high costs.

The original specifications for the system called for it to be developed by an external software company for use by up to 50 portfolio managers in the three departments of the trust division. Within the bank the officer who had first introduced the concept of the portfolio management system became the implementation coordinator. He formed an advisory committee of ten portfolio managers who had the overall responsibility for guiding the development of the system. The technical implementation team from the software company included the team leader and several analysts and programmers.

Due to the presence of a large data base of portfolios it was necessary to employ an advanced technical design, in which terminals were interfaced with a large central computer through a minicomputer. At the time of the design of the system this type of technology was relatively new and unproven, and the software to accomplish this interfacing task had not been developed. The development team underestimated the difficulty of producing the necessary software and this led to an overly optimistic schedule for completion of the project. To make up for some of this lost time the portfolio management system was made available to users in a complete, but not yet debugged form. This did help move the user training program closer to the originally scheduled date, but it resulted in a relatively long periods during which the system failed frequently creating serious user frustrations.

During the training period differences in system usage were extreme. The portfolio managers who made greatest use of the system were the ten individuals on the development team responsible for helping guide the implementation in process. Each of these managers had a terminal next to his or her desk. The implementation coordinator indicated that these individuals used the system intelligently and imaginatively, even when there were technical problems. The coordinator observed the development of a social group among these heavy users of the system. During coffee breaks members of this group discussed reports that had come from the system.

Other portfolio managers made almost no use of the management system during this period. Some of them cited the fact that terminals were not conveniently located near their desks and they would have to disturb others to use the system. Other managers blamed the unreliable performance of the system for its minimal usage. Some individuals were discouraged when the system failed and simply decided to wait until it became fully operational before trying to use it. There was a great deal of frustration expressed by the managers when the system did not work.

Management did take steps to promote the use of the system. The first action was to require system outputs as a standard part of the periodic account reviews mandated by SEC regulations. Instead of indicating that certain reports must be included, specific account review procedures were developed. These procedures contributed to communications as they provided the common frame of reference for the reviews. The presence of the procedures demonstrated to reluctant users that the system was available and was to become institutionalized as a part of the portfolio management process. The action also indicated that management expected portfolio managers to make good use of the system.

Training meetings were also held to help managers who understood the system become skilled users who could employ the system effectively analyzing and managing portfolios. These sessions consisted of several portfolio managers who were enthusiastic users of the system and others who had not displayed much interest. The experienced users demonstrated and discussed the use of the system in the analysis of hypothetical portfolios. They provided thought and ideas for the others and also exerted a form of peer pressure for the less knowledgable users. This technique of training encouraged more uniform use of the system, though there were still managers remaining who were not heavy users. Management also arranged to install a special terminal with a large display screen in a conference room which would allow ten or twenty managers to participate in the same discussion. In addition more terminals were being acquired to facilitate easy access to the system. Finally a hypothetical portfolio system capability was added to the system. This facility made it possible for the manager to construct a hypothetical portfolio and simulate new investment

strategies. Usage of the system doubled in the four months following installation of the hypothetical portfolio function.

Analysis

Table 6.1 contains an analysis of the implementation effort on
the part of the bank, though many of the observations also applied to the original prototype system. Problems arose in a number of the stages of design. Scouting and entry involved the
client, but not the eventual user of the system. One of the basic
ideas was to alter decision style, though there was little management action to prepare for this change. Also, the different
divisions of the bank faced varying environments depending
on the nature of the client and the competition.

A design team of trust investment officers was formed during the diagnosis stage, but it may not have been fully representative of the managers of the bank. The design team apparently ignored the attitudes of potential users who were not
on the team. It appears that decision style and differences
among the divisions and individuals were not considered
further.

In termination use was very high by the design team and
low by others. There was no apparent change in decision style
resulting from the use of the system.

Why was this system only partially successful? The primary
failure here was the lack of consideration of decision style and
different situational and personal factors, and the failure to provide an incentive for use. Benefits to the trust officer did not
offset the personal costs and risks of use. The concept of a
design team was excellent, but the team became isolated. The
external software house did succeed in transferring ownership
of the system to the design team and the investment department
coodinator, but it did not transfer ownership to the potential
users. Special management action after the system was installed was necessary in order to extend system utilization.

Table 6.1 The Implementation of the Portfolio System: Characteristics of Factors at Each Stage

Stages	Technical characteristics	Client action	Factors — Attitudes toward system	Decision style	Personal and situational
Scouting	Need for better portfolio management	Investment manager	Not known	To be changed from security to portfolio-centered	Different divisions
Entry	Desire for on-line response	Investment manager	Not known	To be changed from security to portfolio-centered	Different divisions
Diagnosis	Feasibility of system shown in prototype	Form design team	No apparent consideration	Not explicitly considered	Different divisions
Planning	Design team works on function; interface CRT through minicomputer	Design team to work steadily on system's installation, tailoring	No apparent consideration	Not explicitly considered	Different divisions
Action	Final design of displays, technical problems with interface; converted before functioning	Heavy use by design team forming clique	No apparent consideration	Not explicitly considered	Different divisions
Evaluation	By case writer				
Termination	High levels of use by design team	Design team convinced of value		No apparent changes	Different divisions

What other steps might have been taken during design? During diagnosis and planning a change program could have been developed to show the benefits of the portfolio-centered approach to management. It would have been possible to run hypothetical portfolios and show the result from the new approach to decision makers, such a demonstration should show improved performance for the client. For example, one might have chosen a random sample of trust investment officers to use the new method on hypothetical portfolios to demonstrate to other trust officers the benefits of the new approach.

During the entire design process from the action stage on, the design team could have taken steps to bring in other representatives. They could have used the "county agent" approach (Whisler 1970); with ten people on a team, team members would only have to meet with and solicit ideas from four other individuals to keep everyone involved in the design process. The team members act as county agents discussing the design with other users.

In retrospect it was probably a mistake to try to improve the schedule by installing the system prior to having it completely debugged. The technical characteristics of downtime resulted in complaints from managers about unreliability. Such complaints were reflected in attitudes and willingness to use the system. Not only initial reluctance to begin working with the system had to be overcome but, the historical problem of poor performance had to be countered as well for the trust officers not on the design team.

Forced use of a system for account reviews may result in improved attitudes if the sysem is operating satisfactorily. The strategy could create less favorable attitudes if the system was still not working well.

A number of extensions have been suggested for the system including the possibility of evaluating the performance of the account. However, the design of this aspect of a system would be very difficult because of the varying goals and objectives for the different accounts. If the system is perceived as one that monitors performance and the individual trust officer does not feel that such action is appropriate or can be designed to be fair, lack of use of the system could turn to sabotage. Any extension to this system to monitor performance has the potential for creating extremely negative attitudes and lower levels of use.

In summary, this implementation effort was partially successful as the system is being used and is making a contribution to decision making in the bank. However, there were clearly a number of problems in reaching this point and it does not appear that all of the anticipated benefits were realized by the bank. The idea of demonstrating improved performance for a change to portfolio-centered analysis could still be followed by bank management. Without such a program, the bank may see increased use of the system, but there will probably not be a rapid shift in decision style to a portfolio-centered management approach.

AN EVOLUTIONARY SYSTEM

The organization which developed this system is a major services company with offices' throughout the United States and Europe. This organization places a great deal of emphasis on human assets and employees receive many benefits from this employee-owned firm. The information services department is extremely user-oriented. There are no analysts or programmers and instead the manager of the department refers to his personnel as "implementors." The manager is a senior vice president of the firm and a member of the finance committee, one of the most important committees in the management of the firm.

The vice chairman of the board first suggested the system under discussion. He asked for a small model to predict the impact of an Employee Stock Ownership Plan (ESOP) on the firm. The manager of the information services department wrote a small, 30 to 40 line BASIC program to perform calculations based on projection rules and assumptions provided by the vice chairman. The model was designed to answer questions such as: if we adopt an ESOP, how many shares of stock will be needed by the company in ten, twenty and thirty years? What level of growth is necessary to support the ESOP requirements?

This model raised questions about the impact of the ESOP, which appeared greater than originally anticipated. The information systems department manager and the vice chairman of the board validated the model using a calculator. Even though the projections were surprising, the model did accurately reflect the rules and assumptions which had been supplied. The output of this model was presented to the executive committee which made a decision to adopt the ESOP partially based on this information.

Several top managers who observed the results of the model became excited about the capabilities of the computer and asked if it could be used to make projections on individuals in the firm. Could the system be built for twenty or so "key men" to show their holdings in the company and their worth in ten, twenty or thirty years. Since the professional staff is essential to the firm, such a tool could help retain creative people and point out any inequities in compensation.

As further discussions were held, the functions of this new projections system became increasingly clear. The manager of the information services department developed a rough design for two file records and several formats for screens on a CRT. He gave this to an implementor to develop and update and file maintenance program. The data base was designed to contain the information on employee benefits and to be expandable beyond the 20 individuals originally included. The manager of systems and programming of the information services department and the implementor also loaded stock ownership records for all employees into the data base.

Numerous meetings were held between the implementor, the manager of the systems and programming department and the committee of the top financial staff of the firm to develop the objectives of the "key man" system and the assumptions and characteristics of the projection model. The implementor reviewed the calculations with this committee because the members of the financial staff were often surprised by the results from test runs. During this time the system expanded to include all the employees' stock records and the main user of the system became the treasurer of the company. By this point in the development cycle, the system had evolved from the simple "key man" system to "every person," a comprehensive personnel and benefits application.

Conversion was a gradual process as various parts of the system were completed. Currently staff members in the treasury and accounting area enter and maintain employee records on stock ownership. Occasional requests occur from different executives for projections on individuals. The system is gradually being extended to include all employee benefits data.

The evolution of this system appears to have had an impact on the organization. In this system the gradual development of the application stimulated the participation of users. The system itself was not designed to force a group of individuals in the organization to change their behavior.

The first major change influenced by the system was the adoption of the Employee Stock Ownership Plan. The forecast in the original simple model helped prepare the report recommending this plan to the executive committee. The second major change was in top management perceptions of compensation equity. The firm has over 60 different benefit options. It became clear when compensation packages were projected into the future, that the various options were not equitable compared with perceptions of each individual's contribution to the organization. Thus, the information system has provided data which has helped lead to the development of a more equitable compensation program.

The system also stimulated the creation of a new corporate compensation committee, chaired by the treasurer. The problems of pay and equity combined with a capability in the new system for monitoring employee stock ownership records suggested this change. Since the compensation committee had been previously considered a personnel function, this change does represent a power shift, though it appears to have occurred without major problems. The system has also helped to accomplish a top management goal of moving toward more centralized financial processing for better quality control and efficiency (Lucas 1978b).

Reasons for Success

Individuals interviewed about this system suggested a wide variety of reasons for success.

1. The system's objectives were flexible; specifications were not first cast in concrete, but instead evolved over time.

2. The information services department has a user-oriented philosophy; users are expected to play a major role in the design process.

3. The manager of the information services department believes that and "information system should change the way we look at things." He thinks that the process of developing a system should raise difficult questions about present procedures and suggest new approaches to problems.

4. Management feels that computers are important and should serve the needs of the company; managers are involved in computer-related decisions. Mangement supports information systems development.

5. The information services staff and users exhibit a high level of commitment to the system. There is a mutual excitement and enthusiasm for the application which seems to be contagious in the company.

6. The users and the members of the information services department staff are very well qualified. The implementor of the system, for example, wrote 4,000 lines of debugged computer code in 18 to 20 days.

7. The information services department has extremely good technological tools. It operates a flexible time-sharing system which makes it easy to design and program parts of the system, show them to users and throw them away if they are not correct. The ease of developing on-line applications with this computer system also contributes to the development of systems with a more pleasant interface for the user.

Analysis

This system differs greatly from the previous banking example. Here the system grew from requests by users. There was no external organization (software consultant) involved. The system also did not attempt to change decision style, a difficult undertaking. Management support was more extensive in this case; the system was highly visible.

The framework from chapter 5 can also be used to analyze this evolutionary system. During the scouting stage the system began with a technically simple model at the request of the vice chairman of the board (the client). The situation was extremely relevant and important to the management committee. The entry point was the simply BASIC program. The client provided the rules and helped in validating the model and a good relationship began to develop. Situational factors showed that the system was relevant and there was a high degree of motivation. The user and designer learned together as work progressed. See table 6.2.

Diagnosis was an iterative process; users suggested extensions and the technical factors of on-line operation and a file management system made it easy to develop the application. The review brought more users into the picture, attitudes appeared to be favorable, and users experimented with early versions of the system. The system continued to include the projection capabilities, which made it very relevant to top management.

Table 6.2 The Implementation of the Keyman System: Characteristics of Factors at Each Stage

Stages	Technical characteristics	Client action	Factors		
			Attitudes toward system	Decision style	Personal and situational
Scouting	Request for simple model	Vice chairman of Board initially requested	Not consciously considered	Not consciously considered	Situation relevant to management committee
Entry	Basic program for ESOP	Provides rules, he helps debug	Not consciously considered	Not consciously considered	Situation relevant to management committee
Diagnosis	Revised goals Iterative process to become benefits system	As revised, more financial officers involved designing algorithm	As system expanded, attitudes shaped by implementation approach	Not consciously considered	As revised became relevant to top management
Planning	Resources expanded at each stage-CRT & DBMS	System owner gradually became treasurer	User attitudes influenced through implementation and group discussions of system	Not consciously considered	As revised became relevant to top management
Action	Broader system design and several versions, build data base	Continued mgt. interest. Mgt. provides formulas. Client designs own report	User attitudes influenced through listening; implementation and group discussions of system	Not consciously considered	Expanded to include situation of treasurer
Evaluation	Continued feedback	Managers have faith and enlarge use	Have been integrated	Not consciously considered	Designed for different personal and situational factors
Termination	High levels of use, satisfaction. Treasurer now owner of system	Diffusion to others in organization	Have been integrated	Not consciously considered	Fits various situations and personal factors for users

In the planning stage the system's capacity was expanded during each review, though the changes were gentle. The treasurer of the company gradually assumed ownership of the system. User attitudes were extremely good and the implementor listened and explained to users how their assumptions and rules had been incorporated into the system. The model development was clearly an example of user controlled design. The situational factors in the Treasurer's department are also included in the system through the features added to maintain stock records.

There were also cycles during the action phase. System boundaries were expanded when the data base was constructed. The information services department held continuing meetings with the treasurer and other users. The treasurer had to design his own reports for the system. Favorable attitudes appeared to develop all through this process.

The continuous feedback provided by the gradual design meant that evaluation was undertaken all during the process. There are now further changes occurring, but they are less major.

The termination stage was characterized by high levels of use. The users of the system include many individuals in the organization now and favorable user attitudes exist.

Our conceptual framework of chapter 5 was not followed exclusively in developing this system, but it does help to explain the success of this example of evolutionary design.

COMPARISON

The portfolio management system does not appear to have considered all of the relevant factors during the design process. The desired changes in decision style did not occur, because there was no incentive. The situational variables and differences among departments, because of goals of clients, were not considered. It appeared that the design team forgot to examine the attitudes and importance of other potential users.

Finally the technical problems with the system created frustrations for potential users who attempted to work with the early version. The process of design did involve a design team, but the team became encapsulated and apparently ignored other users. The design team became the sole owner of the system and they did not share it with other potential users. There also appeared to be a lack of diagnoses and planning for installation. Again the attitudes, decision style, personal and situational factors of other potential users were not adequately considered.

The keyman system began with a small effort and strong client support. The information services department did not attempt to change decision style variables with the system. However, they did consider situational and personal factors by adding extensions as new users with different needs were brought into the design process. The client design team grew with the system. Evaluation was able to focus on technical quality because a prototype existed at each stage. After the prototype was validated new features were suggested and added to the system. The development philosophy in this firm is highly consistent with the suggestions in chapter 5. By having user influence to the development of the system the company considers attitudes, decision style and personal and situational factors automatically since users bring these concerns to the design effort. The firm has a responsive computer system and a high quality staff allowing it to develop sophisticated systems in a short time and modify them easily.

Clearly, these two cases do not prove the validity of the implementation framework in table 5.1. However, the purpose of the case discussion is to show the diagnostic powers of the model; the cases suggest that it can be used as a framework for explaining and planning implementation. If the factors in the model and the stages of implementation are consciously considered before designing a system, the chances of successful implementation should be high.

CHAPTER SEVEN
IN CONCLUSION

THIS MONOGRAPH HAS discussed various approaches to implementation. The book adopted use and satisfaction as two important indicators of success. Research on implementation has taken two similar, but divergent paths which have resulted in both process and factor studies. However, these studies are complementary: process studies provide insights while factor studies suggest variables to take into account in implementation. Both types of studies furnish data to revise various theories of implementation.

I proposed a framework in chapter 5 to synthesize the process-oriented approaches to implementation and the factor studies. The process model we chose was a revised version of the Kolb–Frohman approach to consulting which includes the stages of entry, diagnosis, planning, action, evaluation and termination. A review of the literature showed that many of the factors considered in implementation research could be grouped into the categories of technical characteristics, client action, attitudes toward the system, decision style and personal and situational factors.

We also suggested that an implementor has the greatest influence over variables in the order listed above, that is the most influence exists over the technical characteristics of the system and the least on personal and situational factors, at least in the short run.

Three chapters of the book review theories of the implementation of information system and operations research/management science models, process studies of implementation and factor studies. This research supports the implementation strategy suggested by the framework in table 5.1. We need to consider both the process and factors in planning for implementation. Two case studies in the last chapter illustrated how the framework can be applied.

IMPLICATIONS

The most significant findings and recommendations from this monograph are:

1. The implementor should accept the idea that the implementation of information systems or an operations research/management science model is a change activity. Individuals are expected to change their behavior in order to use models and systems. Changes are also likely for work groups and possibly the structure of the organization.
2. The implementor should see that implementation is a *planned* change activity. Implementation should not be treated as a two-week effort beginning with the conversion of a system and ending when a system becomes operational. Implementation begins the day an idea is first suggested for a new system.
3. Consider the stages of the systems design relationship between designers and users and the most important implementation factors at each stage. Remember the importance of the entry point in the organization and the change process during the action stage of systems development. Also consider the significance of the termination stage and the goal of user ownership of the

system. Key factors include the development of a techically sound system, management support and meaningful user involvement, and the development of favorable user attitudes. Also examine decision style and personal and situational variables to determine if they are likely to be significant for a system.

4. Use the framework in chapter 5 to help plan for successful implementation, even to the point of analyzing how each class of user and each individual user will react to a new system. Remember to consider both the task and the process of design.

5. Review the final results and feed them back into the planning for the next implementation effort.

These suggestions will not guarantee successful implementation. However, awareness of the importance and complexity of the implementation process and an explicit plan for it should greatly increase the chances of developing successful information systems.

ABSTRACTS AND SUMMARIES OF SOME OF THE STUDIES DISCUSSED

THE PURPOSE OF this appendix is to provide additional reference information for readers interested in studies discussed in the text. For the studies not contained in this appendix or for further details, consult the references directly.

ARGYRIS 1977. "Management Information Systems: The Challenge to Rationality and Emotionality."

Argyris feels that there are three aspects to formal organizational design that are important in generating work requirement for participants in the organization, including: 1) work specialization; 2) chain of command; and 3) unity of direction.

These properties of the formal organization tend to place employees, especially lower level ones, in situations where they are dependent upon and submissive to their superiors. They experience a very short time perspective and feel low levels of responsibility toward their work. Employees who prefer to experience some degree of challenge, have some control and make decisions will tend to feel frustrated and a sense of psychological failure in this setting.

The impact of task specialization, chain of command, and no need for direction is different at the upper levels. Here the formal design tends to require executives who need to manage a rational world, to direct, control, reward and penalize others and to suppress their own and other's emotionality. Executives with these skills tend to be ineffective in creating and maintaining interpersonal relationships: they fear emotionality. "In the social universe where presumably there is no mandatory state of entropy, man can claim the dubious distinction of creating organizations that generate entropy, that is, slow but certain processes toward system deterioration."

Argyris is concerned that, as organizations become increasingly ineffective, they tend to produce valid information for the unimportant and programmed problems, and invalid information for the important and nonprogrammed problems. His study is concerned with information systems whose usage can alter significantly the way top managers make important decisions. Argyris argues that an information system contributes:

1. To a reduction in the space of free movement since it enlarges the domain to all relevant factors, hence, the expert may ask the behavioral policies, practices, and norms to surface so that their contributions to the problem are made explicit.
2. Psychological failure and double-bind. By centralizing information and planning in an information systems function the result may be to create a world for the local decision maker where daily goals are defined for him, resulting in a sense of psychological failure. Psychological failure occurs whenever someone else defines an individual's goals, paths to the goals, levels of aspiration and criteria for success. Managers aspiring toward challenging work have more responsiblity and thus are frustrated.
3. Leadership based more on competence than on power. Information systems emphasize valid information and technical competence rather than power; information systems also require valid information.
4. Decreasing feelings of essentiality. There will be less need for ambiguity and self-fulfilling prophecies if information is made clear and explicit.
5. Reduction of intra and intergroup politics. A mature information system reduces the need for organizational politics, especially among departments. Departments must provide valid information and abide by decisions made in the in-

formation system. Information systems tend to integrate decisions across departments.

6. New requirements for conceptual thinking. A sophisticated information system will require managers to achieve different levels of intellectual and conceptual competence. There will be less need for intuition and more for a focus on facts.

Argyris argues that if information systems were used effectively, they could actually free the manager rather than restrict him.

He conducted research in an organization which had been managed by intuitive decision making with quantitative financial analysis of a rather simple nature. The researchers observed actual working meetings between managers and operations researchers and analyzed tape recordings of sessions. The following categories of behavior were extracted from the tapes: individual behavior including experimenting, openness, owning, not owning, not open, rejecting and experimenting; interpersonal categories including helping others to experiment, helping others to be open, helping others to own, not helping others to own, not helping others to be open, and not helping others to experiment; and norms including trust, concern, individuality, conformity, antagonism and mistrust.

The results of observing meetings are presented and they fall into two patterns. Pattern A was characterized by a high degree of stating or owning up to ideas. The norm was one of concern for ideas and this characterized seven of the fifteen meetings. There was rare expression of feelings, openness, experimentation, helping others to own up with feelings, etc. Behavior that facilitates or directly inhibits others' behavior or feelings was rarely expressed. There was little risk taking. Individuals rarely expressed positive or negative feelings in the group setting when striving to achieve their tasks.

Under Pattern B, the Management Science team was under stress. There was a high degree of owning up to ideas, however, conformity to ideas became the predominant norm. People were doing more persuading and selling. Helping others was reduced to zero, and antagonism increased. Again, feelings were hardly ever expressed, and there was little experimentation. Managers tended to react in a similar way. "We have two groups who react to stress and tension in ways that will tend to inhibit effective problem solving." The overemphasis on persuasion and increased competition are basically emotional response so that the feelings may be intellectualized.

The client faced with this threat will find other reasons to slowly let the OR groups atrophy, for example, not enough clients will be pursuaded to pay for services. OR team members faced with frustration may not try and coerce others.

Argyris offers some thoughts for coping with these problems. He argues that ideas of mutual understanding and teaching about information systems are probably not effective.

These sessions do not transfer to real situations when individuals are fighting a win/lose game and are under high stress. Suggestions to bridge the two cultures by placing line-managers in MIS groups and vice versa may help. However, these fully educated men or women may enter the arena of conflict of win/lose and use their knowledge about the other side to decrease the probability that that side will win. Unfortunately, all of these are rational solutions to the problem. They may delay conflict, but do not get to the underlying problem.

Team members need to be helped to modify their behavior, that is, to increase their interpersonal competence. Individuals should strive to attain a minimum of psychological conflict and high acceptance of self, to encourage openness, trust, and risk-taking. Openness requires a particular combination of rational and emotional communication. The aim is to create a situation in which the MIS team members can express how they feel and help line executives express them in a similar open manner. The theory is that emotional problems within organizations should not simply disappear when they are not faced; rather they tend to obstruct carrying out rational plans.

BEAN AND RADNOR 1979. "The Role of Intermediaries in the Implementation of Management Science"

This study focuses on the use of intermediaries and their relationship to the life cycle phases of OR/M activities in an organization. Rubenstein has proposed that OR/MS groups which wish to work with production managers would be well-advised to work for industrial engineering departments or intermediaries. The study developed out of a series of case investigations and an attempt to describe different linkages between management science staffs and their clients. After preliminary investigations, the researchers developed two propositions.

1. MS work conducted for specific clients would be more effectively carried out as perceived by clients, when a direct communication link existed between MS-client pairs who had similar functional responsibilities and orientations than would similar projects involving mediated linkages.

2. Conversely clients would perceive their working relationship with OR/MS to be more effective when intermediaries were involved primarily in situations where the functional responsibilities and orientations of the MS client pairs were dissimilar.

These propositions were explored in two large U.S. business firms. Interviews were conducted with fifteen persons in a transitional corporation and 24 persons in a mature corporation. Forty-three critical events were identified and described in detail by clients, including whether or not intermediaries were involved.

Perceived effectiveness of MS/client working relations was measured through interviews. Three indicators of the influence of the critical events on effectiveness were obtained from clients: client satisfaction with working relations, perceived effect on the outcome of specific projects, and perceived effect on interdepartmental relations in general.

The type of interface linking the OR/MS unit to the client was of primary interest. An intermediary was considered to be present in the linkage system when respondents identified personnel other than members of the OR/MS unit as the primary communications contacts or coordinators.

Descriptions of functional relationships and responsibilities were used to ascertain the nature of conditioning variables. Units were considered to be homogeneous when the OR/MS unit was located in functionally-oriented staff groups, such as marketing, research or industrial engineering, and worked on projects for line management in the same functional area. Organizational units were considered heterogeneous when OR/MS units located in cross-functional departments worked with functionally specialized clients.

When differences between companies are ignored, a higher proportion of favorable communications events were reported by clients when the interface was mediated rather than when the direct linkage existed. The outcomes in one company were consistently more favorable than those in the other company. Functional intermediaries are trained in the functional area of business and report to staff groups. Control-oriented intermediaries are trained in accounting and are responsible for coordinating and controlling the allocation of company resources. Intermediaries who are research-oriented working with research-oriented clients have a high proportion of favorable working relationships. The next most favorable relationships occur when functionally oriented intermediaries work with operating managers in the same functional area. The intermediaries whose primary organizational responsiblity was resource allocation and control are associated with a high proportion of unfavorable management science-client relationships.

In summary, the study produced findings which support the hypothesis that the linkage system between OR/MS groups and their clients involving intermediaries who are functionally related to the client unit, but who are organizationally differentiated from them, are more effective than direct linkages. Functionally related intermediaries were also found to be a more effective MS client linkage mechanism than were control-oriented intermediaries. Formal mediated linkages in which the intermediary occupied a position which included elements of both the OR/MS role and the client role but which did not include the resource control activity were clearly more acceptable to the clients than were either the informal direct linkage or the formal third party control-oriented linkages.

BEAN ET AL. 1975, "Structural and Behavioral Correlates of Implementation in U.S. Business Organizations"

The authors developed two success variables, the first is the percentage of all formal projects completed by the OR/MS groups within the two to three year period prior to interviews that were actually used for decision making purposes by the intended user. A second success variable is a composite of five ratings all of which represent perceptions of the OR/MS manager about this group's overall success, its level of support from top management, its level of client support, its project backlog, and the proportion of projects in the portfolio generated by persons external to the OR/MS group.

The figures indicate that perceived success and implementation rates are not highly correlated within industries. The correlation between implementation and success across the entire sample was .32. Some additional explanatory power is gained when the data are grouped by industry. The authors suggest one interpretation is that the norms for perceived OR/MS success differ across industries.

Implementation rate data were obtained from 104 firms. The mean implementation rate was 71.9 percent of all projects that had reached technical completion. The authors present Pearson correlation coefficients between the implementation and the success score for a number of structural explanatory variables in the study. Only two of the direct OR/MS client transaction variables exhibited a significant linear relationship with implementation across the sample. Several other transactions and variables involving OR/MS and non-client personnel were correlated with implementation, for example top management support (.21) and top management interest in OR/MS (.20).

The authors recast their data into a table of results significant beyond the .10 level for the two success variables. The variables are categorized into four groups:

1. Directly controllable within the normal discretion of the OR/MS leader
2. Directly influenced—can be accomplished through direct co-operation between the OR/MS group leader and at least one member outside his group
3. Indirectly influenced—a process leading to the desired conditions can be initiated by the OR-MS groups though the members cannot participate directly in the process once it has been initiated
4. Exogenous variables—created by events lying outside the sphere of influence of the OR/MS group leader and members

An analysis of these results suggests that leaders spending time trying to change the way the organization does things and trying to accommodate OR/MS models plus the organization operating environment will experience higher implementation rates. The other correlates of implementation rate include both structural variables such as formalization of charter, size of budget and level in the hierarchy, and behavioral variables such as the orientation of the group leader and top management support.

Success scores are more strongly correlated with direct transaction variables than with implementation rates. The direction of the relationship suggests that the leaders who spend a high percentage of their time accommodating OR/MS models and outputs in the organizations operating environment and spend a small percentage of their time in selling and administration will be leaders of more successful groups.

It appears that implementation may be less amenable to OR/MS control than success, because the levels of significance of directly controllable and directly influenced variable tend to be higher in the success cases.

The authors also present an analysis of implementation and success by life cycle phases. Though it is interesting to note that the average implementation rates and success scores decline after reaching their maximum values in the organizational phase, the results show interesting shifts in the correlation pattern across the various stages of development.

The overall conclusions are that the data clearly indicate that structural as well as behavioral variables are related to implementation success implying that structural changes as well as attitudinal and behavioral changes may go hand in hand furthering the development of OR/MS in organizations.

BOLAND 1976. "Improving the Problem Definition Phase of System Implementation: A Learning Model Based Strategy"

This study tests an alternative approach for conducting information requirements interviews. The alternative emphasizes the interactive nature of effective inquiry, and realizes that both the analyst and the user must learn from each other during an interview. Learning by both analyst and user proceeds by mutual sharing of expertise, mutual suggestions for potential MIS design, and mutual critiques of suggestions. The interactive approach gives responsibility for teaching, suggesting and critiquing to both the analyst and the user. The analyst does not begin by asking questions, but by revealing information about himself, and allowing the user to do the same. Both the analyst and user come to conclusions and prepare a problem definition statement that merges the information they have revealed about each other.

The proposed technique will be considered successful if it creates a greater amount of mutual understanding between the user and the analyst, if it supports the learning process necessary for the Lewin-Schein theory of change, and if it results in the identification and definition of better problems.

A laboratory study was conducted of a homogeneous group of users and professional systems analysis, in an unstructured two-person problem definition exercise. In this laboratory experiment, user and analyst teams were given a problem finding and solving exercise. Half of the teams used the structured technique of interrogation with the analyst as leader. The other half used structured technique of team design and shared leadership. Task performance and member feelings were monitored. Attitudes of the analyst toward the user and the interaction were analyzed, including satisfaction, trust, openness, realization, interdependence and learning. Attitudes of the user toward implementation of the solutions from each exercise were analyzed. Both users and analysts prepared separate written reports of the results of their meeting. Several panels of graduate students scored the results.

The users were nursing participants who volunteered from a random selection of nurses at a teaching hospital. The subjects were paid for the session. Analysts were volunteers from industrial firms with large, active MIS departments. The task was an MIS planning project for a hypothetical, newly constructed hospital, similar to the one in which the nurses worked. Panels of graduate students rated mutual understanding and nurses rated each team on the nurses' understanding of the analyst and problem identification.

There was no significant difference in the number of problems identified by the interrogative or the interactive analyst or by the groups as a whole. The interactive nurses, however, identified a significantly higher number of problems than the nurses in the interrogative condition. There was a significantly higher idea quality score for the interactive inquiry approach. Also, the consideration of only average or better ideas also showed significantly higher scores for the interactive group. There was no significant difference between the nurses' attitude toward future implementation, perceived benefit from task performance, support by floor personnel or urgency or need for the system's development.

Results of this analysis suggest that in unstructured expert/client situations, problem finding is improved by the use of an interactive inquiry method. Improved problem-finding ability as judged by the quality of ideas generated appears to be accompanied by increased mutual understanding of the participants in the problem-finding process and by increased learning.

CHURCHMEN AND SCHAINBLATT 1966. "The Researcher and the Manager—A Dialectic of Implementation"

The authors use the term implementation to refer to the manner in which the results of scientific effort come to be used by a manager. The authors conclude that there are four distinct roles in the relationship between manager and scientists based on a review of the literature.

1. The separate functionalist thinks of management and re-

search as essentially separate functions. Implementation consists of designing an operational solution which specifies the physical changes that must take place in the organization to accommodate the optimal mathematical solution.

2. The communicator emphasizes the need for creating more understanding on the part of the manager, that is, better lines of communications. A detailed understanding of the manager is not required to have the manager understand the scientist. Communication is a fairly direct process which is independent of the personality of the manager.

3. The persuader views the implementation problem in terms of the manager's personality. The problem is not to provide for the manager's complete understanding of the scientists, but to insure that the scientists understand enough about the manager so that the scientist can overcome managerial resistance to change, alter managerial attitudes, etc. The manager is too busy to develop an understanding of the scientist.

4. The mutual understander takes a synthetic position embracing the position aspects of the previous positions in an effort to bring about the successful union of managers and researchers. The mutual understander argues that science and management can not be separated. If science is to become a method of managing, then managing must become the effort of science.

The authors present a matrix of the four positions, arraying the presuppositions that the manager understands the researcher and the researcher understands the manager against their opposites. Mutual understanding occurs when both conditions have to hold. On the side of management, it calls for an understanding of the politics of decision making and on the side of science, it calls for an understanding of the creative process.

DICKSON AND POWERS 1973, "MIS Project Management: Myths and Opinions and Reality"

The authors asked the MIS experts attending the founding conference for SMIS to rank a list of 34 factors on their importance in achieving a successful project. A study was then conducted of 20 projects in ten firms in the Minneapolis–St. Paul area. The projects were information systems for management; they had to provide information to a manager rather than just process transactions. There are several general findings from the research; the four criteria for success which had been posited for the study were found to be statistically independent, that is, each criterion apparently measured different dimensions of MIS project success. These measures include time, cost, user satisfaction, and computer operations.

Ten factors were found to be significantly related to at least one criterion of project success, though no factor was positively related to completing projects within cost and budget. It is also interesting that user satisfaction as a criterion for success is influenced very differently by other factors than are the tangible criteria: time, cost, and time performance.

The factors are:

1. Participation by operating management in design
2. Organizational level of top computer executives
3. Documentation standards used and enforced
4. Low turnover of project personnel
5. Source of origination of the project, MIS staff or user
6. Length of experience in the organization of project personnel
7. High level programming language used for project
8. High formal education level of project personnel
9. Separation of analysts and programmers for large projects
10. Overall size of the systems staff

With MIS projects the active participation of the actual managers who will use the product is crucial. The following cluster of factors was found related to user satisfaction with project results: the origination of projects by users; the reported clarity of initial objectives and the specificity of user information requirements; the existence of a project team consisting of the managers who used the product; and the manager's perception of the user's project development.

A second cluster of factors represented the management of the project itself. The use of a project control method was not significantly related to any critieria of success. The use of a project control scheme was used as essentially a negative tool to frustrate project leaders since they felt they were helpless to do anything to improve performance without cutting corners.

Finally there was a very great difference between factors MIS professionals believed to be important to project success and what factors in depth studies showed to be related to successful projects.

There are different environments for data processing and generalized MIS projects. With respect to information systems projects, an evolutionary approach to project development should be adopted. This implies a rather fluid development period which takes explicit account of the user's learning process. Follow through of the information systems staff is imperative to the successful implementation of the project. Large omnibus projects covering many functional areas should be avoided and user participation is crucial to the success of the MIS project. However user participation must be taken literally; the actual manager who is to receive and use the products of the project, not staff personnel, should be the participant.

DOKTOR AND HAMILTON 1973. "Cognitive Style and Acceptance of Management Science Recommendations"

The term cognitive style is used to refer to a characteristic, consistent way of functioning that an individual exhibits across perceptual and intellectual activities. The particular style measured used in the experiment is one in which field dependence-independence is the main conceptual component. According to Witkin, "At one extreme is the tendency for experience to be global. The organization of a field as a whole dictates the way in which its parts are examined. At the other extreme, the tendency is for experience to be delineated and structured. Parts of a field are experienced as discrete and the field as a whole is structured." These concepts provide the foundation upon which subjects can be classified as having a propensity to be high analytic (field independent) or low analytic (field dependent).

An individual's cognitive style characteristics are determined both by genetic makeup and by a variety of environmental factors. One crucial element may be the degree of structure in the task. The operations researcher is more often confronted with highly structured tasks than is the average manager. Thus, the operations researcher will tend to have a cognitive style profile which can be characterized as more analytic. Managers, on the other hand, tend to be more heuristic. The authors use these definitions to categorize people into the Churchman-Schainblatt framework based on their cognitive styles and the relationship between the manager and the operations researcher.

An experiment was conducted in three identical sessions. In each case, the test for independence and dependence of field was administered to all subjects. Each was then asked to read a simple business case and assume the role of top management in a given situation. Next, the subject was presented with one of two versions of a consultant's report which were distributed alternately among the subjects according to rank on the Witkin test. After considering the report, each participant was asked to record on a simple questionnaire whether or not he would accept the consultant's recommendation. The authors point out that this measures only acceptance and not necessarily use of the recommendation. There were two groups participating in the study, practicing managers and graduate business students. Report 1 contained all mathematical details and formulas in the main body of the report.

The median cognitive style score was used to divide each of the groups under study into high analytic and low analytic. For the students, the low analytic subject was far more likely to accept their report than the high analytic student independent of the nature of the report. The low analytic student also exhibited a slightly greater tendency to accept the analytic report while the high analytic student tended to accept the general report over the analytic report.

There was little apparent difference in acceptance behavior between the high analytic and low analytic managers. However, the student groups scored significantly higher in the Witkin test than did managers. In fact, the relatively low analytic students were almost as field independent on the absolute scale as the relatively high analytic managers. This result is not surprising since cognitive style charcteristics are strongly influenced by educational background and experience. The highly structured stimuli provided to the subject students through the educational program in contrast to those facing most managers have been shown to strengthen analytic capacity. In addition, the capacity to reason analytically has been shown to decrease over time in the absence of highly structured tasks.

The two groups were matched by selecting students whose test scores most closely approximated those of the managers. Acceptance behavior of the managers and of the matched students differed significantly. Here too the students exhibited a greater propensity to accept the consultant's report than the manager's.

The results indicate the importance of cognitive style and the acceptance of management science recommendations. One also must be careful in using graduate students as surrogates in experiments which are to be generalized to managers.

DYCKMAN 1967. "Management Implementation of Scientific Research: An Attitudinal Study"

Dyckman administered a questionnaire which measured agreement with the Churchman and Schainblatt framework for mutual understanding. A group of managers in a graduate school program at Cornell and operations research professionals in the area participated in the study. Questions were used to classify responses according to the four cells in the Churchman and Schainblatt framework.

It appears that a number of managers were willing to accept the idea that the functions of the researcher and management are separate, because in their view, this is the way it must be, at least in a short run. However, concurrently they feel in need for better understanding of the researcher. Both groups exhibited a strong belief in the need for some type of understanding, but the mutual understanding position did not appear to achieve more agreement than either the persuasion or communication positions. Efficiency can be gained by shifting into the separate functionalist position, though this is likely to be quite dangerous.

The authors discuss Bennis' view of mutual understanding that a good relationship can be produced from building trust and valid communications without recourse to understanding unconscious motivation. Dyckman argues that this may be the operational way to arrive at a mutual understanding.

The results of this study suggest that most managers and researchers viewed the implementation problem as involving more than a psychological aspect. Most of those examined refused to accept this single viewpoint as the most critical means of obtaining effective implementation. Nevertheless, the majority rejected separate functionalist positions in favor of some attempt by one or both parties to solve the problems of understanding their own and the other participants' creative processes. When the experimental statements were made clear, it was found that the mutual understanding position dominated the agree responses.

EVAN AND BLACK 1967. "Innovation in Business Organizations: Some Factors Associated with Success or Failure of Staff Proposals"

Evan and Black administered a questionnaire to 30 graduates of management development programs and 23 employees of two companies. Respondents were asked to select one successful and one unsuccessful written staff proposal, excluding feasibility studies, about which they had first-hand knowledge. A total of 104 descriptions of proposals were obtained. The respondents were drawn from a large insurance company, a prominent engineering consulting firm, and from several companies in various industries.

Fifty-three of the proposals were characterized as successful and 51 unsuccessful. A multiple discriminate analysis was run and seven variables were found to discriminate between successful and unsuccessful proposals. Proposals are more likely to be successful in organizations with a better competitive positions, and with a higher degree of professionalization of staff personnel, of formalization of rules, communication between staff and line personnel, quality of proposals, perceived need for the proposals, and with a lower degree of professionalization of management.

These same factors were used to discriminate between administrative and technical proposals. Organizations characterized by a higher degree of formalization and centralization, communication between line and staff, a quality of proposals, and a higher level of managerial receptivity to change are likely to receive administrative proposals. On the other hand, organizations that are larger in size, have a higher degree of professionalization of management and a larger number of proposals per manager are likely to receive technical proposals.

The results suggest that the results of staff proposals are associated with attributes of the proposal for innovation, attributes of the organizational structure, and attributes of the relationship between staff and line. It also appears that some of the variables which discriminate between successful and unsuccessful proposals also discriminate between technical and administrative proposals.

GALBRAITH 1979. "A Change Process for the Introduction of Management Information Systems: A Successful Case"

This paper describes a case study of an implementation of computer systems in a large manufacturing company with many plants throughout the country. The plants are decentralized and functionally organized. There is a sequential work flow and material moves from the preparation stage to the fabricating stage and finally to the finishing stage which prepares the final product. Management had been dissatisfied with the return from this part of the business. Several other firms are the acknowledged and low-cost producers while this firm is at the industry average.

A group trying to automate the factories "rode" in on new machines; computers and new technology were implemented with the new machines. The systems group was able to attach computers as add-on to new machines and other capital requests and the plants found it difficult to resist since they wanted the machines and capital additions. This strategy got the technology into the plants.

The in-plant development of new technology as a change strategy consisted of two parts. One part was set of practices which differentiated new machines from the rest of the plant in order to protect them from short-run time orientation and pressures for current production. The second part was a set of practices which were intended to integrate the new unit into the rest of the plant, and facilitate the speed of new ideas and practices.

The machines to which the computers were attached were not made part of the plant organization. Instead, the two major operations, fabrication and final preparations were placed in a single department under a brand manager. These new innovations and machines were regarded as "a management island," isolated from the short-run pressures and counter-forces which might prematurely eliminate the new innovation. A second, critical feature of the stratagem was financing the new technology and computers from corporate headquarters rather than the plant. This allowed the plants to request to pursue their own capital projects and the add-one did not occur at the expense of the plant's own projects. The plants did not request computers and were not penalized financially for adopting them. The programming and development staff were also provided by the research group. The plant did not have to divert its own resources, though it could not control the extra resources.

Collectively, these practices isolated and protected the computer technology to allow for experimentation, development and breathing space, which were needed to prove the worth of the new practice. The technology was made to work and controlled from corporate headquarters until successful. Then the burden of proof shifted to the plant to demonstrate why the technology would not work.

To diffuse the computer the information systems corporate group employed several other practices including in-plant development teams, a local plant capability in computer technology, and diffusion of the management island. Collectively, these practices created permanence and constitute a basic technological transfer method.

The first approach was the development of teams. Technical members from corporate headquarters and from the local technical group operating managers and local maintenance and engineering staff work on the island. Technical experts teach the practitioners about computers and information systems, and the managers teach the technical staff about operations and local differences.

The second technology transfer practice was the establishment of a local capability in computer applications. After the project was completed and the corporate staff groups left, the unit served as a local repository of technical knowledge to assist in the spread of new practices. The unit also served as a link between corporate research and planning.

The management island was staffed with younger managers. The young managers tended not to have perceptual sets, and were enthusiastic supporters of the program. These managers were moved to other positions in the plant after two or three years and the diffused managers then requested computer systems for machines in their departments. The graduates of the management island program became internal advocates facilitating diffusion.

The process has been regarded as successful; the first machine to which computers were added was installed in 1967, another in 1969, and another in 1973. Interviews with 25 managers indicated unanimous support for the process control computers and they are now being requested widely. The results are mixed with respect to the usefulness of management information. Positive responses came from managers with a direct experience with the information. The younger the manager and the less the manager's previous experience in the function, the more enthusiastic the response. Negative responses come from those with no direct experience with the experimental unit. The technology transfer, in summary, is working. The local technical units have been established and sustained. The applications are spreading and in a second plant three new projects have been initiated in units other than the management islands.

The process is consistent with findings that top management support and adequate resources are needed for successful implementation. Management creates a climate in which there is an acknowledged problem, provides adequate resources to groups proposing solutions, and assists the organization in the development of a management island. Management also provides financial and psychological support to newly-trained managers. This continued involvement of top management is one of the factors accounting for the success experienced so far. The research unit has also demonstrated a considerable political acumen. They have gained top management support and established linkages with other staff groups.

This process of differentiating a unit from the rest of the organization to invent new practices is a common change strategy, but it creates the need to integrate the process and to aid diffusion.

GIBSON 1975, "A Methodology for Implementation Research"

This article discusses a case study in a bank in which the researchers were participant observers. A questionnaire was administered as a part of the project and it confirmed distinct clusters of attitudes among officers which could be predicted on the basis of biographical data. An index of "banker"–"marketer" dimensions was developed by assigning weights to variables expected to predict attitudes towards banking, a computer and the bank as a place to work. The best such independent variables turned out to be department worked in, age, experience in the bank, whether or not the respondent had a degree and whether or not he had participated in the bank's orientation program for potential officers.

For agreement on questions like "When it comes to using computers in this bank a little knowledge is a dangerous thing" and "Computers are at their best when used for routine operation," the definition of the categories, marketers and bankers is not clear. The bankers appear to be more conservative and they tend to choose other bankers as their colleagues on a sociometric choice question while marketers chose other marketers.

The authors observed many communications problems in the bank which had implications for implementing a model being developed. What began as a phase of joint development between the builders and users of the model, because of the environment, evolved into a virtually turnkey project.

The basic conclusion was that behavior and organizational forces effect the outcome of implementation. The author cautions that one should be careful in making generalizations about factors which are thought to insure or contribute to implementations success. In this case the key figure could not be heavily involved in the design of the model. Gibson suggests that we need to conceive of implementation as a process of influence in organizations.

GINSBURG AND RAMSEY 1975. "Field Centered Implementation"

The authors described two primary design strategies: designer-centered and user-centered. The authors describe a process which has been successful at Wells Fargo Bank called field-centered which assumes that neither party can adequately describe the other's real needs. In the particular example described, the process included multiple roles—the designer's roles, the designers as users, and the users as designers. This approach has been successful in providing designs which require little additional change, in facilitating implementation, and in reducing user training. The authors describe three themes which they feel facilitate implementation:

1. Users and designers are learning-process-oriented rather than end-product-oriented.
2. Neither users nor designers abdicate their responsibility for implementation.
3. Experience with an early version of a model is provided.

They point out Ackoff's paradox that a user-centered approach will not work if the manager does not know what he or she needs. In the designer-centered approach, the designer often places too much emphasis on technology. The elements of field-centered approach are designers, requesters, users, clients, peer group, the environment, present effect of past events, the present effect of anticipated or future events and the present effect of other elements.

The principles of field-centered design include:

1. The here and now—the user's present problem
2. Concrete and not abstract
3. Experiential—a model for the user's actual problem
4. Iterative and evolutionary to solve one problem at a time
5. User involvement in design
6. Conflict resolution
7. Testing of the design

The field-centered approach has a high level of designer and user interaction built in affording an opportunity for developing a close working relationship. The authors summarize the benefits of their approach on a single project. The model accomplished the user's objectives; the product was timely and had the confidence of the user.

The user's influence served as a deterrent to highly sophisticated and overly complex models. The MS group was afforded the opportunity to assist in the quantification of subjective and intuitive data and to address questions leading to the development of other models for that user.

GINZBERG 1979. "A Study of the Implementation Process"

The author argues against system use as a basis for measuring successful implementation. Instead, he feels that the appropriate dependent variable is the user's belief that his goals for the project have been met. Ginzberg utilizes the Lewin–Schein theory of change containing three phases on unfreezing, moving, and refreezing. In particular, Ginzberg adopted the Kolb–Frohman model of the consulting process which includes the stages of scouting, entry, diagnosis, planning, action, evaluation, and termination.

The major hypothesis investigated is that the success of an MIS implementation effort would be positively correlated with the quality of the implementation process. That is, successful projects would show better resolution of the issues presented at the various stages of development than would unsuccessful projects.

A questionnaire was developed and administered to managers and management scientists. The subjects tried to reconstruct the process of implementation through the questionnaire. Statements described conditions congruent with the resolution or non-resolution of various implementation issues. The questionnaire was developed through the help of a panel of five change agents. The dependent variables included a single question on overall satisfaction and a scale measuring the level of adoption. Users tended to have different perceptions of the implementation process making it necessary to analyze each user's score independently for a given project.

Data were collected for twenty-nine projects in eleven organizations. There were three levels of complexity for the projects: low, medium, and high. An example of a complex project would be simple standard accounting routines, while the most complex group would be model-based management systems.

There was markedly lower agreement between the manager and management scientist about the conduct of the implementation process where the user was dissatisfied. An initial test of the major hypothesis was performed by comparing the reported handling of the seven process stages between those users satisfied with the outcomes and those not satisfied. By far, the greatest difference occurred in the termination phase. The same pattern of differences was not found for the consultants, which is consistent with earlier findings that consultants seemed generally unable to differentiate between successful and unsuccessful implementation efforts. The data do not support the contention of the stages of the process will differ in relative importance across technology types, that is, the level of complexity of the system.

The author suggests that the management scientists should view his other role that of a change agent and should be sensitive to conditions in which his other skills and the project requirements are not well matched.

HAMMOND 1974. "The Roles of the Manager and Management Science in Successful Implementation"

The author focuses on applications which permit a specific individual or a group of individuals to reach an important decision as opposed to a system designed to help an organization to make recurring decisions. Hammond argues that the manager is not really economic man and his goals are often different from those of the organization. It is important to know how a manager thinks about the decision problem and Hammond presents a perceptual model of the forces influencing a manager's decision-making, including the decision problem, related data, external forces, and management science.

Hammond suggests there are three characteristics which are obstacles to the use of management science:

1. Improper expectations about the purposes of the analysis and of each party of the other
2. Strongly held preconceptions about the nature of the problem or about a preferred alternative
3. A sharp differentiation between the characteristics of the management scientist and the decision maker which precludes an effective interface

Hammond also discusses the concept of functional fixedness when individuals are too inflexible in their approach to a problem or a solution. He presents a table highlighting the differences between goal-orientation, time horizon, inherent expertise, interpersonal style, cognitive style, problem definition, method of validation of analysis, and degree of structuredness required for the manager versus the management scientist.

Hammond suggests that a new role for management science is needed to place it in the position of augmenting, stimulating and otherwise assisting the reasoning of the manager instead of finding a solution. The measure of successful implementation then becomes the degree to which the manager's problem solving is augmented and stimulated rather than whether the conclusions of the management scientist are adopted.

HUYSMANS 1970. "The Effectiveness of the Cognitive Style Constraint in Implementing Operations Research Proposals"

The Implementation problem in the experiment was for an OR proposal which was technically adequate with explicit recommendations. The research was relevant to the problem at hand and was superior to the managers' present policy even when transition costs are considered. The experiment examined the impact of cognitive style on the acceptance of the OR proposal. The experimental task consisted of a series of problem trials presented in two sequences. The task was an extended version of the newsboy problem and it was the same for all six groups, differing only in the setting of parameter values. The subject played the role of the president while the four manager's roles were simulated. Only teletype communications and limited vocabulary were allowed. Each firm operated for a total of 14 periods over three sessions. Subjects were classified according to two typical ways of reasoning: Analytic or Heuristic.

There were two implementation strategies and the president had to deal with two heuristically oriented and two analytically oriented, simulated managers created through scenarios. One implementation strategy aimed at gaining the subjects' explicit acceptance and the other at gaining an integral understanding of the operations research proposal.

The subject's adoption or rejection behavior was measured largely on the basis of his or her marketing and production decisions, using a scoring formula which is based on the difference between the actual decision and optimal decision. Measures were also devised for the messages sent to classify them into analytical, functional, organizational and other categories.

Hypothesis 1. Analytic Subjects will achieve a higher degree of implementation than heuristic subjects and have at least as high a degree of acceptance if the accounting manager uses the explicit understanding approach in presenting the OR proposal.

Hypothesis 2. Heuristic and analytic subjects who receive the integral understanding approach will reach a higher degree of implementation of the OR proposal than the heuristic subjects who receive the explicit understanding approach.

Hypothesis 3. Heuristic subjects will suppress analytic arguments in their communications if the explicit understanding approach is used.

A series of 35 experiments was conducted and the first two hypotheses were strongly supported by the experimental evidence. The experimental evidence also indicated that acceptance of an OR proposal by no means guarantees its implementation. In fact, over half of those who did not implement to a measurable degree had at the same time accepted the optional proposals for one or more products. The data do not, however, support the hypothesis that heuristic subjects suppress the analytic arguments in their communications when the explicit understanding approach is used.

The main hypotheses of the study can be summarized as:

1. Cognitive style may operate as an effective constraint on the implementation of OR recommendations.
2. The operations researcher may achieve implementation by taking this implementation constraint into account.
3. When the cognitive style propensity or the operations researcher and manager do not agree the manager may discard the OR proposal. The research recommendation will not be implemented no matter how persuasive and intuitively appealing the OR arguments may be.

Huysmans could identify no single factor that had strong predictive power for adoption behavior.

The explicit understanding approach involved the inclusion of the formulas to support the research findings. The integral understanding approach stressed general appreciation for an integral understanding of the research. The author indicates that one conclusion from the study is that the integral understanding approach is not an easy means of creating a true understanding between the analytic researcher and the heuristic president. In the experimental situation they could prevent the alienation of a heuristic subject from an analytic operations researcher by de-emphasizing the difference in cognitive style. However, the price of this strategy is that the subject does not receive the full fruit of the research unless the researcher commits himself to a long range, post-research involvement with the manager's problem.

MAHER AND RUBENSTEIN 1974. "Factors Affecting Adoption of a Quantitative Method for R & D Project Selection"

The company in the experiment was primarily concerned with the manufacture and supply of capital goods. The Division was responsible for the execution of research programs which were planned for and financed by operating divisions of subsidiary companies. An experimental project evaluation technique was developed based upon a Monte Carlo simulation program. There were five phases in the study:

1. Data collection to develop an appropriate model
2. Development of a Monte Carlo simulation program for R & D Project selection
3. Debugging and training in the use of the model
4. Incorporation of the model into the exploratory research project selection-decision process
5. Assessment of the willingness of participants to adopt a model as a part of organization or routine through the use of a questionnaire

The model is based on an approach by Hertz which systematically combines probability estimates associated with possible outcome values, that is, risk analysis.

Three factors have a relatively strong positive degree of association with an individual's willingness to adopt the model on a routine basis. These are: 1) perceived value to an individual of the data generated by the model; 2) the perceived appropriateness of the information, for example, techncial versus commerical, considered by the organization as a result of implementation; and 3) the perceived value of changes in project's research strategies.

Two factors have a weaker but positive association with willingness to adopt: 1) the perceived appropriateness of the model's mechanical features, for example, the number of variables considered and the mathematical operations performed on the variables; and 2) the perceived compatibility between the decision process with and without the model (the more compatible, the more willing to adopt.)

Four factors involving the participants use of new or existing communications channels were affected by the use of the model: 1) the perceived need to develop new communications channels; 2) the perceived need to increase the use of existing communications channels; 3) the perceived use of new communications channels; and 4) the perceived use of existing communications channels. Two factors were also affected, but to a much lesser degree. These are: 1) the perception of the information considered by the organization; and 2) the perceived changes in project research strategies.

Two factors related to an individual's assessment of the value of the data generated: 1) the individual's perception of the appropriateness of the input data prepared for the model; and 2) an individual's perception of the legitimacy of the input data prepared for the model.

The authors present a descriptive model of the factors associated with willingness to adopt and of the changes attributed to the use of the model. The implications suggested by the authors are related primarily to the use of selection models. It appears that the assessment of the value of the output data generated is more important than changes in the organization's decision process. However, such organization process changes are important aspects in determining an individual's willingness to adopt such a technique. The introduction and use of an R & D project selection techniques can have a marked effect on individual users and their behavior. The information seeking behavior of individual users is likely to be affected as well as the strategies associated with their research activities. These changes can be anticipated and planned and may have a strong influence on an individual's decision to continue using such a technique. Such changes should be anticipated in the introduction and use of the technique.

MALCOLM 1965. "The Need for Improvement in the Implementation of OR"

Malcolm states that the difficulty in implementing OR includes the assessment of costs of implementation and successful performance. Malcolm feels that OR should be approached as a continuum of effort starting with basic research and leading up to implementation of development. He recommends a procedure for establishing an OR program and a criteria for initial project selection.

There has been a split between individuals interested in making ideas work and in those interested in a more comprehensive or accurate mode (theory versus application). Too much concentration on theory leads to highly sophisticated models, generally applicable only to lower levels of operation which are not of real interest or understood by management. Too much concentration on applications can get the analyst overinvolved in the particulars of a given problem without the authority to resolve it. The author concludes that adaptation of the solution to meet the practical consideration should be made during the course of an OR study before implementation is recommended.

There are three solutions suggested to solve the problem of implementation:

1. Add an implementation function to the OR group responsibility
2. Create a management system design and implementation function to take over and implement OR results
3. Rotate OR practitioners into line positions to implement their policies and recommendations.

MANN AND WILLIAMS 1960. "Observations on the Dynamics of a Change to Electronic Data Processing Equipment"

This study is a descriptive field study over several years of the adoption of electronic data processing system by a major electric utility. The firm had no prior computer equipment. There were two accounting divisions in the company with over a million customers in each. The jobs of the divisions were to handle billing and records, and control customer contacts on service and payment. There were 800 employees in the central office and 1,000 in geographic offices. An EDP system was developed to maintain customer accounts which were previously on tab equipment.

The authors identified the following phases of the change

1. Consolidation of customer requests

2. Consolidation of internal visual customer records with a master record replacing eight records in five locations

3. Centralization of record keeping and data processing

4. Consolidation of records of all customers regarding accounting

5. Required organizational changes (including transfer of func-

tions among employees and a major reorganization in the accounting division, work sections and departmental line reorganization, new departments created, and a level of management added). There was little chance to stockpile; the firm had to keep offering service.

The stages of growth observed were:

1. Stability and equilibrium before the change

2. Preliminary planning

3. Detailed preparation

4. Installation and testing

5. Conversion

6. Stabilization

7. New equilibrium after change

The system was announced in October of 1953 and the computer arrived in October of 1956. The conversion started in January 1957 and in 1958 the initial disturbances were over and they began to establish permanent tasks.

Management used the development of the system as an excuse to review the organization. Was this very broad rethinking a good strategy for change? Could any of the changes be made without the system?

Some of the bookkeeping functions from the district were transferred to the central office and all customer contacts were centralized in sales. Sales seemed to relegate the change to a lower position. The accounting division reacted well because of participative management in that division according to Mann and Williams.

The company tried to handle job elimination through attrition and opened bidding for jobs throughout the division. During the changeover all the jobs were classified as temporary. There seemed to be the lack of a concept of what the organization would be like. Instead of deciding what kind of organization is desired and building it, the organization reacted to change. The presence of the temporary job classifications increased uncertainty for the workers.

During the transition there were heavy time demands, deadlines and overloads. The supervisors needed a mix of technical, human relations and supervisory skills. Employees were concerned over their ability to adjust, as well. There was heavy overtime and great uncertainty created by the temporary job classifications.

The sales department had more trouble adjusting than accounting, probably because of less involvement. Also the computer was controlled by accounting. Liaison representatives were used, however, there were communications problems between sales and accounting. There was limited sharing of information for sales. The system was sold, not in terms of customer service, but for improving accuracy and reducing cost. There appeared to be general mistrust of information. Users were not ready for a new form of information presentation and some individuals developed informal information systems of their own.

There was a loss of job control for sales; the system interfered in the way of customer service. There were many problems with errors and securing corrections which created negative attitudes. A consultant's study of errors found that they were not unusual for a system of this type. This report forced sales and accounting to work together to resolve the errors.

Final job assignments did not go too smoothly. Employees were forced to fill the jobs from the highest grades down. Supervisors tried to find the best fit assignment, though it was very difficult to resolve and no manager wanted to have bad candidates. It was hard to maintain morale, especially since lower than expected job grades and pay resulted from the change.

The authors concluded that the change to the equipment accelerated the level of formalization in the organization, reduced the status of some decisions, provided less autonomy for individuals and work groups, and created more deadlines. There was greater interdependence and more coordination required and there was a shift toward centralization, contrary to management's goals. Many of the jobs replaced were routine and tedious, and the authors felt there was some job enlargement. There was also greater identification of errors and more responsibility for the employee: the unsuccessful worker was clearly in the spotlight.

MANLEY 1975. "Implementation Attitudes: A Model and Measurement Methodology"

Manley developed a model of critical factors in implementation in the form of a mathematical scoring model for predicting group resistance to change. This problem involves mathematically describing resistance in terms of significant variables which when properly related provide a measure of probability of implementation success due to client behavior. A questionnaire was used to gather data to score and validate the model.

An experiment was conducted for a hypothetical MS recommendation for change for a group of school teachers. Variables that were altered were the degree of chief executive school district superintendent support expressed for the project, the level of client involvement required for project implementation, and the degree of relevance of the project to different members of the client group.

Major hypotheses of the study were:

1. Variations in the behavioral response of client to an OR/MS project can be measured and used to provide an indicator of the probability of implementation success.

2. Differences in the level of chief executive support cause significant variations in resistance.

3. Differences in the degree to which clients are required to become personally involved in the implementation of a project will cause significant variation in success.

4. Differences in the degree of relevance of the product will affect the degree individuals support or resist it.

The author presents a descriptive model of the OR/MS project implementation decision process in the form of a flowchart. He also discusses the factors which create resistance in the client implementing an OR/MS project.

Manley develops a multiplicity of scoring models which can be used to predict client resistance to OR/MS implementation. Key variables include the degree of project complexity, the amount of management support, etc. The model also employs a weighting factor with respect to the relative importance of each external variable. The model includes an intermediate variable which is used to describe an individual client's attitude orientation toward each factor in the model. The dependent variable is defined as a measure of client behavior that can be logically interpreted as equilibrium resistance or support for a specific OR/MS diffusion project.

A literature search was used to develop factors important in the implementation process. Semantic differential units were developed, and ratio scale values of the weights developed, and external variables scaled. The experimental design to test the model used four sub-groups at high and low values for four different variables; 153 subjects responded to the questionnaire. The change was a hypothetical, but completely realistic proposal, for a modified payroll procedure. The teachers perceived the relative importance of the factors in the following order of decreasing importance:

1. Relative urgency for the new method to solve a real problem

2. Relative importance of the new method to individuals who will be affected by it

3. Degree of top level support

4. Relative simplicity of the new method

5. Amount of personal participation required to implement the new method

The calculated model score correlated at the .32 and .34 level with questions directly related to attitude variables about the chance of success and personal effort expended to help install the new system. The model seemed to show logically consistent results.

MITROFF 1975. "Toward a Theory and Measure of Total Problem Solving Performance"

Mitroff presents a qualitative model of human problems solving which consists of four nodes connected by arcs. The nodes are

1. Reality problem situation

2. Conceptual model

3. Scientific model

4. Solution

Each phase of the model influences every other phase, so each phase possesses its own unique characteristic features which the others do not have.

Conceptualization is a process which is governed by deep intuitive and dialectical thought processes. Model solution aims at the reduction of uncertainty while conceptualization aims at its increase.

Model solution is concerned with the usual type I and type II errors while conceptualization is concerned with the error of the third kind, or solving the wrong problem.

The measure of successful implementation, successful problem solving, is not adoption action or any one of a host of other variables that is uncorrelated with problem solving. However, successful problem solving means more than just removing the immediate problem at hand, it also increases one's conceptual model building and solution capability.

Every one of the difficulties connected with implementation is as much a problem of faulty conceptualization and model building and model solving as it is faulty implementation per se.

Mitroff suggests that one of the most thorny problems connected with problem solving is the source of problems, by whom and how are problems made known? Information systems and management science usually attack existent well defined problems without conceptualizing.

Mitroff closes with a quotation from Akoff that problems and solutions are conceptualized as snapshots of a moving process. Problems and solutions are in constant flux—solutions to problems become obsolete, even if the problems to which they are addressed do not.

MITROFF, NELSON, AND MASON 1974. "On Management Myth-Information Systems"

This paper relates an experiment in which an information system presented data through myths or stories. The authors argue that "An organization's factual data, no matter how precise or accurate they may be, are not information unless they are integrated into one or more of the key motives which define the symbolic nature of the organization."

The essence of dialectical information systems (DIS) is conflict. DIS are designed to present the strongest possible arguments on an issue between at least two of the strongest opposing views or positions on that issue. The concept of DIS rests on the basic assumption that a decision-maker would be better able to formulate a richer policy decision as a result of witnessing an intense debate between opposing policy positions or experts, rather than by witnessing agreement between them. The notions of stories and the idea of drama were central to DIS because they are not only constructed to present the most compelling and logical case for each position, but they are also constructed to present the most psychologically compelling or affective case for each position. Each side in the dialectic does its best to convince the manager that its view or story is the one that is correct.

The authors desired a series of experiments: one involving a computer program called "Beat the Computer" and the second involving a series of exercises called "Freud." The first exercise was designed to move the subjects attitudes toward dialectical thinking and the second to induce the participant to think dialectically.

"Beat the computer" involved playing a game under conditions of uncertainty. Subjects were instructed to pick the row in each matrix on the screen which they believed would give them the largest payoff. In order to help them form a strategy, subjects had the opportunity to listen to two experienced experts of the game, Smiley and Grumpy. Smiley represented a max-max or optimistic game strategy and Grumpy represented a max-min or pessimistic game strategy. The game was rigged so that if the subject followed either Smiley's or Grumpy's strategy exclusively, they stood no change of winning. The purpose of rigging was to set the stage for the emergence of third expert, synthetic Sara. After losing Sara pointed out that Smiley and Grumpy were too locked into their positions.

The Freud program begins with an introductory statement to highlight the difference between dialectical and conventional thinking. The program presented a one-way and a two-way position and a series of attitude questions which the respondent answered. The computer responded with a critical message that either praised or attacked the subject's response depending upon how far the subject was from the pure two-way position. Positions in accord with the two-way or dialectical thinking were praised, and others were attacked.

All thirty subjects responded to a seven-point Likert questionnaire that pertained to dialectics and the value of seeing both sides of an issue. There was a significant shift between pre- and post-tests, all of which were in the direction indicated by the dialectic theories. In particular, the subject strengthened their beliefs that an intense argument on two strongly opposing sides of an issue was useful in clarifying points, good teachers make you unsure about the way of looking at things, for every issue there are always two equally creditable but opposing and contradictory sides, vague assignments are usually more interesting than well defined ones, paintings are as real and as good a means of representation as are photographs, non-scientists should be able to speak out on issues and poets are sometimes a better judge of mathematical problems than are mathematicians.

NARASIMHAN AND SCHROEDER 1979. "An Empirical Investigation of Implementation as a Change Process"

This paper presents a conceptual model of the change process and the results of a multiple case-study in eight business organizations. In each participating organization, a single decision problem was selected and data were collected about it through questionnaires and a set of semistructured interviews with OR/MS staff and management.

In all eight cases, the scientists' intervention resulted in more formal methods, a systems point of view, an explicit treatment of uncertainty, and a more comprehensive analysis of relevant alternatives. These represent the usual thrust of management science intervention efforts. The scientists' major involvement and impact was on the evaluation and choice phase of decision-making. Most of the scientists appeared to be subscribing to the "separate functionalist position" of Churchman.

Changes in the decisionmakers' perspective depended on whether the scientist worked closely with them or not. A close working relationship generally created greater understanding of the problem, and ability to use a more structured approach, etc. These changes induced other changes in decisionmakers, such as a more favorable perception of management science.

Data from Likert questionnaire items were subjected to factor analysis, followed by a nonparametric correlation analysis. This analysis showed that the working relationship and technical validity variables were the most important factors affecting the changes in decision processes of decisionmakers.

The authors revised their conceptual model based on the analysis of the data. The revised model has three important characteristics of management science intervention: interaction/working relationship, operational knowledge, and logical analysis. Operational knowledge of the scientist affects the technical validity and organizational validity of recommendations, and the scientist's ability to communicate with decisionmakers. High operational knowledge of the scientist instills in the manager's trust and confidence in the OR recommendations.

Organizational factors play a secondary role in influencing changes. They define what management science can attempt to do in terms of model analysis. Particularly important are the availability of relevant information, time and resources available for the scientist's task, top management support and involvement.

The authors conclude that

1. Change processes are complicated and marked by a series of interdependent influences. Multiple causality exists among influencing factors.

2. The conceptual model postulates a hierarchy of changes, suggesting it would be fruitful to adopt a staged approach to affecting change.

3. If implementation is viewed as a process of effecting change in decision-making behavior, model installation is not absolutely essential for implementation to occur.

4. Factor analysis shows that technical validity and working relationships are important in terms of change.

5. Working relationships between the scientist and the manager are extremely important.

6. A perception of payoff on the part of the manager and informed use of a model are essential to the creation of favorable perceptions of management science.

7. Organization factors play a secondary, though important, role as determinants of change.

NEAL AND RADNOR 1973. "The Relation between Formal Procedures for Pursuing OR/MS Activities and OR/MS Group Success"

The authors interviewed subjects in 108 companies including the Manager of the OR/MS function. Independent variables in the study included whether the group had an operating charter or not and the level of procedural elaboration used in pursuing an OR/MS project. Dependent variables included the project implementation rate and the level of the success of the group on several indicators. Intervening variables measured included whether OR/MS leader had a professional or organizational orientation, the extent to which top management was interested and involved in endeavors, and various environmental factors that might conceivably affect the relationship between procedures and success, the most important of which being the stage of the OR/MS group, the relative size of the group, and the degree of diffusion of OR/MS talent throughout the organization.

A large number of tables and chi-square statistics are presented to support the predictions made by the authors. The principal argument of the study, that procedural elaboration and the success of an OR/MS group are positively related, proved to be significant. The professional or organizational orientation of the OR manager and top management knowledge, interest and involvement in OR/MS exhibited significant relationships with group success, but not the elaboration of procedural guidelines.

Of the several environmental factors considered, three proved to have similar associations with both procedural elaboration and group success, including the age of the group, its relative size, and the diffusion of OR/MS within the organization.

These preliminary findings indicate that the proceduralization of OR/MS activities does have a positive effect on success of OR/MS groups. However, it is still very likely that proceduralization rather than causing success may be an indicator of a successful group.

RADNOR, RUBENSTEIN, AND TANSICK 1970. "Implementation in Operations Research and R&D in Government and Business Organization"

The authors suggest three viewpoints of implementation:

1. A transition process taking place between successive stages in a work-flow pattern

2. A special case for organization change or adaptation

3. A continuous process during all phases of a project

The authors have developed a general set of eleven factors from their research on the environment of implementation. The eleven items are:

1. Recognition of the need for project

2. Willingness of the individuals in receiving units to interrupt ongoing work to handle something new

3. Technical mismatch in understanding the specifications of the project

4. Mismatch in understanding objectives of the project or task

5. Pre-existing relations of trust or confidence between the parties to an implementation transaction

6. Degree of involvement in stages of a project

7. Self interest

8. Urgency

9. Perceived threat

10. Level of managerial support

11. Appointed time at which a management commitment is made to the project

These eleven variables are linked in a series of thirteen propositions about the relationship among independent and dependent variables.

Based on their experiences the authors feel that the type of organizational goals are extremely important environmental variables affecting implementation. They also suggest there are several summary variables which appear to be of key importance:

1. Nature of the client-researcher relation

2. Level and type of top management support for the research activities

3. Type of organizational and external environment in which the research activity is pursued

Some data are presented using the number of organizations as the unit of analysis to test the relationship among these variables. In general, better client relations were associated with fewer implementation problems and top management support. These two variables together seemed to be critical in analyzing problems of implementing OR/MS activities. The data suggested that the maintenance of good client relations was relatively more important than management support in alleviating implementation problems.

The data collected by the researchers, though not clearly specified, support the hypothesis that higher levels of organizational goal operationality lead to operation of the OR/MS activity based upon results of implemented projects in instances of analytic implementation strategies. Organizational goals appeared to be related to implementation strategies. Based on the data and discussion, the authors suggest that there are several methods for bringing about successful implementation.

1. Assuring that there is a clear and recognized need for the results at the time the project is undertaken

2. Involvement of the ultimate user of the results early in the process and maintaining communication throughout the project

3. A focus of the direction or strategy of the project in an individual or small group that can review progress and make decisions about changes in direction or level of effort

4. Having top management support and enthusiasm

5. Allowing or encouraging researchers to follow projects into applications areas and to make careers there if they so desire

RADNOR, RUBENSTEIN, AND BEAN 1968. "Integration and Utilization of Management Science Activities in Organizations"

This article describes the experiences of the authors in 66 U.S. companies. The paper describes the type of personnel involved in O/R and management science activities, and the qualifications of these individuals.

The paper is primarily descriptive and discusses the location of OR/MS groups in the organization. There are also examples of a number of OR operations that have been disbanded. The implications are that OR/MS is best removed from R&D or engineering at a central location, possibly related to financial areas, to top management or to planning. Certain problems seem to arise for the OR/MS activity in the financial area.

Top management support appears to be one of the key variables affecting the likelihood that OR/MS activities will be successful. In the sample in this paper, awareness and interest concerning OR/MS at the very highest levels in large companies was generally rather slight. There was a strong relationship between the fortunes of the sponsors and the OR/MS groups. Poor reception of OR/MS activities by user groups was described for the following reasons:

1. Poor project results

2. Use of highly technical terminology

3. Unsatisfactory experience with outside operations research consultants

4. Unorthodox or unbusinesslike appearance of OR personnel

5. Identification with a highly specialized functional area

6. Inability to demonstrate cost-effectiveness

7. Method of allocating project costs

8. Differences in planning horizons

It appears that implementation problems have plagued OR/MS rather constantly over the past ten years. While the attention given to liaison and coordination has increased, whether the liaison and coordination effort has been carried through to the implementation stage for individual projects is a question which requires further study. One major problem appears to be the personality conflict between the operations researcher and clients.

RUBENSTEIN et al. 1967. "Some Organizational Factors Related to the Effectiveness of Management Science Groups in Industry"

The authors present a general model relating the events that occur in the history of an OR/MS activity, the conditions under which it functions, and in its effectiveness. These conditions are:

1. Level of managerial support

2. Client receptivity

3. Organizational and technical capability of the OR/MS persons or groups

4. Organizational location of the activity

5. Influence which the group and its leadership could bring to bear in the organization

6. Reputation of the activity within the organization

7. Adequacy of the resources allocated to the activity

8. Relevance of projects undertaken to the needs of the organization

9. Level of opposition to the OR/MS activity within the organization

10. General perception of the level of success of the activity in the organization

New organizational activities seem to pass through several stages in their birth and development and these variables differ according to the stage.

The four stages in the life history of an OR/MS activity are

1. The pre-birth phase in which people in the organization are expressing ideas on the possibilities of having such an activity

2. Introductory phase in which management is granted a charter to perform OR work

3. Transition phase in which management has a longer term commitment to OR/MS activities

4. The maturity phase in which management has accepted the OR/MS group function as a permanent part of the organization. Progress in the latter phases may be terminated or reversed by the death of the activity

Interviews indicated three freedoms necessary for OR/MS groups. The first is the freedom to select projects, the second, the freedom to gather data, and the third, the freedom to implement proposals. There are three factors which influence success for the preliminary data:

1. Management understanding of the OR discipline

2. A personal relationship between the OR/MS supervisor and those using the function

3. The results of previous projects

SCHULTZ AND SLEVEN 1975. "Implementation and Organizational Validity: An Empirical Investigation"

The authors conducted a literature search to identify potential variables related to implementation. The 57 variables relevant to the implementation of OR/MS models in an organization were reduced and grouped into 14 general headings. Other factors were developed from reviews of the literature. Approximately 100 Likert type statements were generated based on 81 input variables and semantic differential scale was also developed. The scales were assembled and pilot tested on MBA students and then revised. The results were correlated with various dependent variables as well.

A group of 106 questionnaires was administered to management personnel at a metal manufacturing company. A factor analysis on the results produced understandable factors including: performance, relations, changes, goals, support and resistance, plant and re-searcher interface, and the urgency for results. The correlation of the Likert scores and the semantic differential are generally high. Cor-relation analysis indicated that a substantial number of attitudinal variables correlated significantly with five dependent variables. The results are discussed in some detail.

The authors suggest a quantitative measure of fit between the model and the organization. There are some preliminary implications for policy. First it can be useful to emphasize the personal benefits of a model or innovation. Top management's support is important as well as goal congruence between organizational tasks and the model. The relationship between the client and the researcher is important to implementation success. On the other hand, change and interper-sonal relations do not seem to be very critical and may be factors to be de-emphasized in implementation.

SCHULTZ AND SLEVEN 1977. "An Innovation Process Perspec-tive of Implementation

The authors present a model of the adoption process based upon Robert's eight stage model:

1. Problem perception

2. Awareness

3. Comprehension

4. Attitude

5. Behavioral intention

6. Trial

7. Adoption

8. Performance evaluation

Empirical explanatory variables are arrayed against these stages of adoption to show what research has been performed and also to indicate the importance of these variables in various adoption stages. The model is presented as a series of hypotheses to show which variables are important longitudinally in the implementation process. In the model, stages 1 through 3 are considered to be a cognitive field; 3 to 5 an attitude field; and 5 to 8 in the behavioral field.

"For our purpose it is not so important to include all these complexities as it is to explore the appropriateness of the general adoption model applied to implementation. At a minimum, such models show how rejection of the innovation can take place at any stage."

SHAKUN 1972. "Implementing Management Science Via Situational Normativism"

The author suggests that an approach is needed to create the mutual understanding of Churchman. In his model, situational normativism leads to mutual understanding, there is a feedback loop between the two. Mutual understanding leads to the unity of science and management which in turn leads to implementation and to organization and system development.

Situational normativism is a descriptive, normative approach to decision making and policy science. The methodology begins with a descriptive behavioral model of real world decision situation in terms of the participants, their values, objectives and goals and the decision rules which determine existing outcomes. The description of the existing system provides the basis for constructing a mathematical model of that system for normative purposes. Existing system constraints were not viewed as fixed. In fact, the solution process (normative) involves a search for change in these constraints as well as a search for a solution satisfying change to constraints.

Situational normativism involves a search by the manager and a scientist for a synthesized situational frame of understanding within which solutions to the decision situation problem can be found. Under situational normativism the long range involvement between the researcher and the manager may be required as suggested by Huysmans. The analytic operations researcher has much to learn from a heuristic manager about heuristic reasoning the latter has much to learn in the form of analytic reasoning. Mutual learning and adaptation including changes provided by situational normativism provide a basis for relaxation of the cognitive style constraint.

The author presents examples of how this approach has worked, for example, he suggests that the dialectical approach discussed by

Mason and Mitroff could be useful in the search by scientists and managers for a synthesized situational frame of understanding. Various examples of past research are cited to show how situational normativism is consistent with them.

SOUDER et al. 1975. "An Organizational Intervention Approach to the Design and Implementation of R&D Selection Project Models"

This paper describes the use of a questionnaire-based method in the design of R&D project selection models. The authors present a model of implementation in which the dependent variable is willingness to adopt a selection model. The willingness is influenced by model characteristics with an intervening variable set of organizational factors and personal decision variables. The general design methodology is to find out what specific variables constitute the basic variable set. Then considering these specific variables and the intervening variables in a causal chain the model builder can adjust the model by manipulating its characteristics. The authors present a questionnaire and an example is given of utilizing this approach in an organization for a project selection model. A predictive equation was developed for willingness to adopt.

To use a predictive equation for a particular project selection model the score for that model for each specific factor is first attained by administering questionnaires to persons familiar with that model. These specific variables scored within each of the three basic variable categories are averaged to obtain basic variable scores for the predictor equation. These predictive equation scores cannot be used for highly accurate results because of the error attached to the dependent variables. However one is interested in direction and the relative rankings of the models.

An example is given of an application of the technique in a hierarchical organization. Two other applications are presented in less detail without the results of the questionnaire. The total design methodology consists of a two part sequence. In the first part significant organizational and personal decision variable systems that influence willingness to adopt are identified. In the second part, a suitable model form is selected from among several candidates on the basis of the model's impact on the significant variables. A series of questionnaires is given in the first part of the design in order to define the significant variable systems. Another series of questionnaires is given in the second part to aid in selecting a suitable model from among several potential candidates. The second series of questionnaires is used to collect input data for predictive equation which can be used to forecast the acceptability of the willingness to adopt for particular model forms. In one of the interventions the subject's willingness to adopt a project selection model was reversed from negative to positive.

STABELL 1975. "Design and Implementation of Decision Support Systems: Some Implications of a Recent Study"

The author begins by surveying Gerrity's methodology for the design of decision support systems (DSS). Gerrity lists eight design principles:

1. DSS design should provide for evolutionary change of the decision system.

2. Ultimate users should be kept involved, aware, and contributing to the design process.

3. Explicit decision models based on human decision behavior should be utilized in the design process.

4. The design should aim at providing accessible programmed operators for the manipulation of data and models in the system.

5. The design should employ explicit design search and generation mechanisms that encourage broad consideration of alternative designs.

6. The design should employ explicit mechanisms and models for predicting ultimate DSS behavior.

7. The design should aim for reasonable flexibility.

8. An explicit decision control system should be designed as one component of the system.

Basically, the difference between normative and descriptive models of decision-making behavior is meant to define the objective of a specific DSS development effort. The change in how decisions are made should be evolutionary and not revolutionary. What emerges is a view of development which involves computerizing the information processing primitives of the decisionmaker. Over time, it is hypothesized that the manager will evolve programmed procedures composed of these primitives which incorporate the desired changes in the decision-making process.

The paper describes the characteristics of a decision support system designed for portfolio management by Gerrity. "Gerrity found that the average session length was 60 minutes, the average number of reports requested per session was 13 and that no function accounted for more than 21% of total function use. In contrast, data on actual operational use indicated much shorter sessions (average length five minutes), fewer reports requested per session (three reports on the average), and much heavier use of a limited number of the ten functions available on the system (two functions account for approximately 80% of total system use)."

Comments from Stabell's interviews suggest that the portfolio system provided a snapshot of previous decisions as opposed to basic data for decision making. It was used more as a reporting tool than as a tool for the investment process.

Stabell presents a critique of Gerrity's methodology; he suggests there are three problems with the approach;

1. Low manager capacity for change

2. Non-operational nature of the desired change

3. Designer-centered methodology

The managers had problems integrating information provided by wide variety of sources. They tended to reply heavily on a limited number of sources in a relatively unintegrated and compartmentalized fashion. Low development of manager understanding of the information environment is one barrier to an evolutionary change in decision-making behavior. The main definition of normative behavior was that the investment process should become more portfolio-oriented, however, little was said about the dimensions or characteristics of a portfolio-oriented decision-making process. For example, training was limited to how to use the functions available on the system. This approach produced a very weak link between the functions implemented and the normative goal of the system. The functions implemented were more responsive to the needs of the existing decision-making process than considerations of the normative decision process. There also problems with the database for research. The quantitative estimates provided by research analysts were viewed as inexact, unreliable, and not up-to-date. The involvement of the users in the process was passive rather than active.

Stabell proposes some extension to Gerrity's model to improve the chances for successful implementation. The manager-user should be involved much more as an active agent in all phases of design and implementation process. The design should not be for a user, but rather with the user.

SWANSON 1974. "Management Information Systems: Appreciation and Involvement"

Swanson tests a model in which a priori involvement coproduces MIS appreciation which coproduces inquiry involvement. The inquiry involvement of a manager consisted of his cooperative involvement with the inquiry process or use, the a priori involvement of a manager consisted of his cooperative involvement with MIS design implementation, and operation processes. The MIS appreciation of a manager consisted of his manifold beliefs about the relative value of the MIS as a means of inquiry.

Swanson used an inquiry system for activity reporting in a large engineering department of an electronics manufacturer. This system gathered data on the planned and actual work activity of the group members and made it available to management. There were two files available for inquiry by management, one containing work activity for the most recent thirteen weeks and the second is an eighteen-month summary of work activity. A large number of unique reports could be easily derived from the system.

The inquiry history file was used as a source of an indicator of inquiry involvement. A research questionnaire was constructed to obtain indicators of MIS appreciation and a priori involvement. The inquirer was judged to be active on a given working day if he or she entered one or more queries. The index between inquiry involvement was the relative frequency of these active days during the thirty days sampled. MIS appreciation was defined as a simple average of sixteen individual items on a questionnaire.

Because of the generally low level of a priori involvement on the ten items, "no involvement" was scored as zero and any involvement was scored as one for computing a scale. There were thirty-seven usable responses out of forty-six questionnaires distributed.

The direction of covariation was as expected for all of the variables. The covariation between a priori involvement and inquiry involvement also appears to be explained by the intervening variable of MIS appreciation. In fact, knowledge that a manager was unappreciative was almost sufficient to imply complete non-involvement. In a second case, knowledge that a manager was appreciative was almost sufficient to predict involvement in some form, but nothing can be said in which form. Thus, for any particular form of involvement, MIS appreciation appears to be a necessary, but not sufficient condition.

The author raises the question as to what determines the type of involvement experienced by a user. He speculates that the extent to which an individual perceives himself or herself to be a change agent in the organization might lead to a priori involvement, which is a process of making inquiry involvement possible for others.

VERTINSKY 1972. "OR/MS Implementation in Valle, Colombia, S.A.: A Profile of Developing Region"

Vertinsky employed two complementary strategies for research, a community study, and a longitudinal case study of implementation. The first part of the research was a survey of 200 Colombian companies, and all foreign companies with 100 employees or more. Forty firms were drawn from the Colombian population and five were selected from the foreign group, the latter to control for cultural variation. The president or general manager of each firm was interviewed to explore the implementation process. This research was followed by a longitudinal case study of the important OR project in the region, a health services planning project.

The research questions in the study were designed to obtain a profile of OR/MS in the region, to determine the characteristics of management involved such as attitudes and the original structure and decision-making processes, and to examine the process of innovation and how management technology was adopted. External influences in response to environmental conditions were also examined and there were very few OR/MS practitioners in the area though a number of programs had brought external consultants into the country.

The basic need for hiring an operations researcher was to routinize procedures and to collect or process data, or it was a "power play" in the company. The main task for which OR/MS specialists were hired concerned restructuring information systems. In all cases, management attempted to reduce environmental uncertainties, especially in semicompetitive markets (six out of eleven cases). In five out of eleven case studies, the consultant was hired by a group in management to strengthen their organizational power or to resolve an intra-organizational conflict. The authors developed a theory of implementation which they tested including the following variables: the attitudes of executives, the organizational structure and modes of decision making, the receptiveness or resistance to change, and the compatability of the national outlook with the value system of the executive. Receptiveness or resistance to change was related to attitudes, risk-taking and uncertainty in management situations, curiosity and search drive.

The various scores were summed to provide cumulative score with receptive, indifferent, and resistance as the major points. A dichotomy was developed to explain possible consequences of alternative values systems or cultures. A continuous culture is based upon a linear, teleological concept of the world. The world is considered a consistent sequence of cause-effect relationships. Management Science techniques are consistent with the continuous culture, for they provide a formulation for these teleological processes.

A discontinuous culture is based upon a compartmentalized point of view of the world. Experiences are limited in time and space. Relationships are particularly heuristic and diffused and MS/OR techniques would be foreign in such a culture. It appears from the data presented that no company was classified in the continuous cell. The authors feel that executives who are generally receptive to innovation are likely to adopt OR/MS techniques. However, adoption would be partial and temporary and it is likely to disintegrate when the OR consultant leaves the organization.

An important attitudinal variable often neglected in the image of OR. In many cases, management expectations were unrealistically high and consequent evaluation of OR was uncritical and unrealistic. In other cases, the inflated image or OR lead to a backlash of overcritical evaluation, suspicion, and disbelief.

Analysis of organizational charts in the study often discovered a system geared to maintain an organizational static equilibrium, a system of checks rather than a system of controls. It is difficult under these circumstances to create a consensus in the organization to undertake an innovation. The tendency to compartmentalize also limited innovation.

VERTINSKY ET AL. 1975. "A Study of OR/MS Implementation as a Social Change Process"

This research involved the administration of a questionnaire to individuals, both OR/MS practitioners and client-managers, in a variety of businesses. A total of 115 responses were obtained and interview data were also collected from the companies. The questionnaire assessed managers' perception of the role of OR/MS in the organization and were factor analyzed. Various correlation analyses are described.

The interview results suggested a motivational model of OR/MS implementation (adopted from Lawler). This model consists of expectancy, which is the manager's expectation that the implementation of OR/MS will lead to task accomplishment or performance. Expectancy is influenced by the manager's self esteem, that is his beliefs about his ability to cope with and control his environment and his personal or observed experience given similar or identical stimulus situations. Another type of expectancy refers to the manager's belief that task performance based on the use of OR/MS will lead to desired outcomes or payoffs. The third variable, valence, refers to the manager's degree of preference or indifference to the kinds of payoff contingent upon performance achieved through the use of OR/MS.

The expectancy theory approach hypothesizes that these three variables, the two expectancies and valence combine to determine the manager's use of OR/MS. The authors present a mathematical formulation of the model and summarize their conclusions:

1. OR/MS solutions relating to significant social change tend to mobilize counterforces aimed at reversing or at least containing these changes.

2. Forced implementation of solutions does not necessarily lead to changes and may in the long run be counterproductive.

3. Changes in management approaches depend on the intensity of dissonance stemming from a manager's perception of conflict between his management style and OR/MS.

4. Use of OR/MS when solutions do not significantly affect the function or structure of the organizational unit may result in long run social change if certain conditions are met.

5. The establishment of trusting, informed relationships with

OR/MS practitioners depends on both the level of motivation for use of OR/MS in the organization and the interpersonal competence of OR/MS practitioners.

6. The manager's quantitative aptitude increases the likelihood of successful and informed use of OR/MS.

ZAND AND SORENSON 1975. "Theory of Change and the Effective Use of Management Science"

Zand and Sorenson review several theories of change including problem-centered, personality-centered, and multi-factor. The authors adopt a process theory of change based upon the work of Lewin. Change consists of a process with three phases: unfreezing, moving, and refreezing.

Unfreezing occurs by means of disconfirmation, psychological support and occasionally guilt or anxiety. Moving is a conceptualizing problem concerned with acquiring information about relevant forces. Unfreezing occurs through confirmation, psychological support, and heightened confidence. The authors test six hypotheses concerning success in the various change stages and implementation success. For each of the three phases, if forces are favorable to that phase, for example, unfreezing, the unfreezing should have a high positive correlation with success. If forces are unfavorable, then resistance to unfreezing will have high level of correlation with success. The other hypotheses are symmetrical. Some 154 out of 391 members of a chapter of management science organizations completed a mail questionnaire.

The instrument was carefully designed; eleven experts were interviewed to provide two critical incidents from their experience, one successful and one unsuccessful. Content analysis was conducted of the eleven interviews. A content unit is easily identified, large enough to have meaning and small enough not to have multiple meanings irrelevant to the subject under investigation. Of the 406 content units, 201 units were relevant to the phases of the change theory. Elimination of duplication left 51 satisfactory units. Seven behavioral scientists familiar with the change theory independently classified each of the 201 content units into change phases. If a unit was assigned to one of Lewin's change phases, the behavioral scientists sorted it into one of seven possible levels of favorableness. A questionnaire was developed and pretested.

The final questionnaire asked respondents to consider two critical incidents, one exceptionally successful and the other unsuccessful. Ten weeks after the initial mailing, a retest questionnaire identical to the first was mailed to 39 randomly selected subjects. Test-retest reliabilities were from .69 to .97 for the 23 usable returns. The correlations between each phase of change and level of success had signs in the predicted direction and were highly significant at the .01 level. Indices of force favorable to each change phase correlated positively with success and indices of forces unfavorable to each phase correlated negatively with success. Indices of favorable forces for each phase correlated positively with each other and indices of unfavorable forces for each phase correlated positively with each other as predicted.

The authors suggest that unfreezing may be a complex and potentially unstable phase. Management scientists and users attempt to identify the problem, estimate its severity and assess the need for change. At the same time, the parties are negotiating relationships with each other. Strong reservations and resentment during unfreezing are likely to cause great difficulties during moving. Moving is favored when unfreezing, the need for change, is recognized by the users. Refreezing and the level of success, circularly reinforce each other. The results provide strong support for the Lewin theory as applied to the implementation of OR/MS models.

REFERENCES

Ackoff, R. K. 1967. "Management Misinformation Systems." *Management Science*, 14(4):B147–56.

Alloway, R. 1975. "Application of a Contingency Theory of Temporary Management Systems to the Creation of Computer-Based Systems." In P. Keen, ed., *The Implementation of Computer-Based Decision Aids*. Cambridge: MIT Press.

Alter, S. 1975. "Great Eastern Bank: A Portfolio Management System." Unpublished case.

Allison, Graham. 1971. *Essence of a Decision: Explaining the Cuban Missile Crisis*. Boston: Little Brown.

Anthony, R. 1965. *Planning and Control Systems: A Framework for Analysis*. Cambridge: Division of Research, Graduate School of Business Administration, Harvard University.

Argyris, C. 1971. "Management Information Systems: The Challenge to Rationality and Emotionality." *Management Science*, 17(6):B275–92.

Bean, A. S., R. D. Neal, M. Radnor, and D. A. Tansik. 1975. "Structural and Behavioral Correlates of Implementation in U.S. Business Organizations." In R. L. Schultz and D. P. Slevin, *Implementing Operations Research/Management Science*. New York: American Elsevier.

Bean, A. S. and M. Radnor. 1979. "The Role of Intermediaries in the Implementation of Management Science." *TIMS Studies in the Management Sciences*, 13:121–37.

Bean, A. S. and C. D. Shewe. 1976. "Management Information Systems Implementation: A Cross-Validation of the Attitude-Behavior Relationship." Unpublished paper.

Bjorn-Anderson, N. and B. Hedberg. 1977. "Designing Information Systems in an Organizational Perspective." *TIMS Studies in the Management Sciences*, 5:125–42.

Boland, R. J., Jr. 1976. "Improving the Problem Definition Phase of System Implementation: A Learning Model Based Strategy." Paper presented at the Implementation II Conference, University of Pittsburgh.

Boland, R. J. Jr. 1978. "The Process and Products of Systems Design." *Management Science*, 24(9):887–98.

Churchman, C. W. and A. H. Schainblatt. 1965. "The Researcher and the Manager: A Dialectic of Implementation." *Management Science*, 11(4):B69–78.

Churchman, C. W. and A. H. Schainblatt. 1967. "On Mutual Understanding." *Management Science*, 12(2):B40–42.

Dickson, G. and R. Powers. 1973. "MIS Project Management: Myths, Opinions and Realities." In W. McFarlan, R. Nolan, and D. Norton, eds., *Information Systems Administration*. New York: Holt, Rinehart and Winston.

Doktor, R. and W. F. Hamilton. 1973. "Cognitive Style and the Acceptance of Management Science Recommendations." *Management Science*, 19(8):884–94.

Duncan, R. B. and G. Zaltman. 1975. "Ethical and Value Dilemmas in Implementation." In R. L. Schultz and D. P. Slevin, eds., *Implementing Operations Research/Management Science*. New York: American Elsevier.

Duncan, W. J. 1974. "The Researcher and the Manager: A Comparative View of the Need for Understanding." *Management Science,* 20(8):1157–63.

Dyckman, T. R. 1967. "Management Implementation of Scientific Research: An Attitudinal Study." *Management Science*, 13(10):B612–20.

Evan, W. and G. Black. 1967. "Innovation in Business Organization: Some Factors Associated with Success or Failure of Staff Proposals." *Journal of Business*, 40:519–30.

Galbraith, J. R. 1979. "A Change Process for the Introduction of Management Information Systems: A Successful Case." *TIMS Studies in the Management Sciences,* 13:219–33.

Gerrity, T. P. 1971. "Design of Man-Machine Decision Systems: An Application to Portfolio Management." *Sloan Management Review.* 12(2):59–75.

Gibson, C. F. 1975. "A Methodology for Implementation Research." In R. L. Schultz and D. P. Slevin, eds., *Implementating Operations Research/ Management Science*. New York: American Elsevier.

Ginsburg, S. and C. Ramsey. 1975. "Field-Centered Implementation." In P. Keen, ed., *The Implementation of Computer-Based Decision Aids*. Cambridge: MIT Press.

Ginzberg, M. J. 1974. "A Detailed Look at Implementation Research." Cambridge, MIT Center for Information Systems Research.

Ginzberg, M. J. 1979. "A Study of the Implementation Process." *TIMS Studies in the Management Sciences,* 13:85–102.

Gorry, G. A. and M. S. Scott Morton. 1971. "A Framework for Management Information Systems." *Sloan Management Review*, 13(1):55–70.

Hammond, J. S. 1974. "The Roles of the Manager and Management Scientist in Successful Implementation." *Sloan Management Review*, 15(2):1–24.

Harvey, A. 1970. "Factors Making for Implementation Success and Failure." in "Free-for-All." *Management Science*, 16(6):B312–21.

Hickson, P. J., C. R. Hennings, C. A. Lee, R. E. Schneck, and J. M. Pennings. 1971. "A Strategic Contingencies Theory of Interorganizational Power." *Administrative Science Quarterly*, 16(2):216–19.

Hoyer, Rolf. (1980). "User Participation: Why Is Development So Slow?" In H. Lucas et al., eds., *The Information Systems Environment*. Amsterdam: North Holland.

Huysmans, J. H. B. M. 1970. "The Effectiveness of the Cognitive Style Constraint in Implementing Operations Research Proposals." *Management Science*, 17(1):92–104.

Kilmann, R. and I Mitroff. 1976. "Qualitative Versus Quantitative Analysis for Management Science: Different Forms for Different Psychological Types." *Interfaces* (February 1976).

Kolb, D. A. and A. L. Frohman, 1970. "An Organizational Development Approach to Consulting." *Sloan Management Review*, 12(1):51–65.

Larreche, J. C. 1979. "Integrative Complexity and the Use of Marketing Models." *TIMS Studies in the Management Sciences*, 13:171–87.

Lawler, E. E. and R. J. Hackman. 1969. "Impact of Employee Participation in the Development of Pay Incentive Plans: A Field Experiment." *Journal of Applied Psychology* 53(6):467–71.

Lucas, H. C., Jr. 1974. *Toward Creative Systems Design*. New York: Columbia University Press.

Lucas, H. C., Jr. 1975a. *Why Information Systems Fail*. New York: Columbia University Press.

Lucas, H. C., Jr. 1975b. "Methodologies for Research on the Implementation of Computer-Based Decision Aids." In P. Keen, ed., *The Implementation of Computer-Based Decision Aids*. Cambridge: MIT Press.

Lucas, H. C., Jr. 1976. *The Implementation of Computer-Based Models*. New York: National Association of Accountants.

Lucas, H. C., Jr. 1978a. "Unsuccessful Implementation: The Case of a Computer-Based Order-Entry System." *Decision Sciences* 9(2):68–79.

Lucas, H. C., Jr. 1978b. "The Evolution of an Information System: From Key-Man to Every Person." *Sloan Management Review*, 19(2):39–52.

Lucas, H. C., Jr. 1978c. "The Use of an Information Storage and Retrieval System in Medical Research." *Communications of the ACM*, 21(3):197–205.

Lucas, H. C., Jr. 1979. "The Implementation of an Operations Research Model in the Brokerage Industry." *TIMS Studies in the Management Sciences*. 13:139–54.

Lucas, H. C., Jr. and R. B. Plimpton. 1972. "Technological Consulting in a

Grassroots, Action-Oriented Organization." *Sloan Management Review*, 14(1):17–36.

McCoubrey, C. A. and M. Sulg. 1976. "ORMS Implementation at Converse Rubber." *Sloan Mangement Review*, 17(2):63–76.

Maher, P. M. and A. H. Rubenstein. 1974. "Factors Affecting Adoption of a Quantitative Method for R&D Project Selection." *Management Science*, 21(2):119–29.

Malcolm, D. G. 1965. "On the Need for Improvement in the Implementation of OR" *Management Science*, 11(4):B48–58.

Manley, J. H., 1975. "Implementation Attitudes: A Model and Measurement Methodology." In R. L. Schultz, and D. P. Slevin, eds., *Implementing Operations Research/Management Science*. New York: American Elsevier.

Manley, J. H. 1976. "Implementing Change in Very Large Organizations." Paper presented at the Implementation II Conference, University of Pittsburgh.

Mann, F. and L. Williams. 1960. "Observations on the Dynamics of the Change to Electronic Data Processing Equipment." *Administrative Science Quarterly* 5(2):217–56.

Mason, R. D. and I. I. Mitroff. 1973. "A Program for Research on Management Information Systems." *Management Science*, 19(5):475–87.

Mitroff, I. 1975a. "On Mutual Understanding and the Implementation Problem: A Philosophical Case Study of the Psychology of the Apollo Moon Scientists." In R. L. Schultz and D. P. Slevin, *Implementing Operations Research/Management Science*. New York: American Elsevier.

Mitroff, I. 1975b. "Toward a Theory and Measure of Total Problem Solving Performance." Cambridge, MIT Center for Information Systems Research.

Mitroff, I. I., J. Nelson, and R. O. Mason. 1974. "On Management Myth-Information Systems." *Management Science*, 21(4):371–82.

Mumford, E. and O. Banks. 1967. *The Computer and the Clerk*. London: Routledge & Kegan Paul.

Mumford, E. and D. Henshall. 1979. *A Participative Approach to Computer Systems Design*. London: Associated Business Press.

Mumford, E. and T. B. Ward. 1968. *Computers: Planning for People*, London: B. T. Batsford.

Narasimhan, T. R. and R. G. Schroeder. 1979. "An Empirical Investigation of Implementation As a Change Process." *TIMS Studies in the Management Sciences*, 13:63–84.

Neal, R. D. and M. Radnor. 1973. "The Relation between Formal Procedures for Pursuing OR/MS Activities and OR/MS Group Success." *Operations Research*, 21(2):451–74.

Pounds, W. F. 1969. "The Process of Problem Finding." *Industrial Management Review*, 11(1):1–20.

Radnor, M. 1979. "The Context of OR/MS Implementation." *TIMS Studies in the Management Sciences*, 13:17–34.

Radnor, M., A. H. Rubenstein, and A. S. Bean. 1968. "Integration and Utilization of Management Science Activities in Organizations." *Operations Research Quarterly*, 19(2):117–41.

Radnor, M., A. H. Rubenstein, and D. A. Tansik. 1970. "Implementation of Operations Research and R&D in Government and Business Organization." *Operations Research*, 18(6):967–91.

Rubenstein, A. H., M. Radnor, N. Baker, D. Heiman, and J. McColley. 1967. "Some Organizational Factors Related to the Effectiveness of Management Science Groups in Industry." *Management Science*, 13(8):B508–18.

Scheflen, K. C., E. E. Lawler, and R. J. Hackman. 1971. "Long-Term Impact of Employee Participation in the Development of Pay Incentive Plans: A Field Experiment Revisited," *Journal of Applied Psychology*, 55(3):182–86.

Schein, E. *Process Consultation: Its Role in Organization Development.* 1969. Reading, Mass.: Addison Wesley.

Schultz, R. L. and D. P. Slevin. 1975. "Implementation and Organizational Validity: An Empirical Investigation." In R. L. Schultz and D. P. Slevin, eds., *Implementing Operations Research/Management Science.* New York: American Elsevier.

Schultz, R. L. and D. P. Slevin. 1977. "An Innovation Process Perspective of Implementation." Krannert Graduate School of Management, Purdue University Working Paper No. 601.

Shakun, J. 1972. "Management Science in Management: Implementing Management Science Via Situational Normativism." *Management Science*, 18(8):367–77.

Shein, E. 1965. *Organizational Psychology.* Englewood Cliffs, N.J.: Prentice-Hall.

Simon, H. 1965. *The Shape of Automation for Men and Management.* New York: Harper & Row.

Souder, W. E., P. N. Maher, N. R. Baker, C. R. Shumway, and A. H. Rubenstein. 1975. "An Organizational Intervention Approach in the Design and Implementation of R&D Project Selection Models." In R. L. Schultz and D. P. Slevin, eds., *Implementing Operations Research/Management Science.* New York: American Elsevier.

Stabell, C. B. 1975. "Design and Implementation of Decision Support Systems: Some Implications of a Recent Study." Stanford: Graduate School of Business, Stanford University.

Swanson, E. B. 1974. "Management Information Systems: Appreciation and Involvement." *Management Science*, 21(2):178–88.

Vertinsky, I., R. T. Barth and V. F. Mitchell. 1975. "A Study of OR/MS Implementation as a Social Change Process." In R. L. Schultz and D. P. Slevin, eds., *Implementing Operations Research/Management Science.* New York: American Elsevier.

Vroom, V. 1964. *Work and Motivation.* New York: Wiley.

Zand, D. E. and R. E. Sorensen. 1975. "Theory of Change and Effective Use of Management Science." *Administrative Science Quarterly*, 20(4):532–45.

INDEX